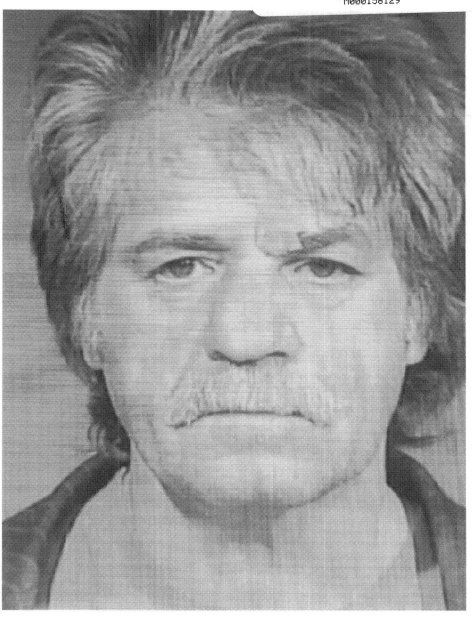

April, 2010—DWI

The Black SHEEP

The Fittest / Unfittest Bar Owner In New York

TOM M^cGRATH

WITH JARED BEASLEY

Disclaimer: The authors have tried to recreate events, locales and conversations from memories of them. In some instances, the authors may have changed the names of individuals and places, some identifying characteristics and details such as physical properties, occupations and places of residence, in order to maintain individual's anonymity.

For information about special discounts for bulk purchases, or for permission requests, please email tomrunningman@aol.com

Interior and cover design by Craig Anthony, craiganthony83@gmail.com

ISBN: 978-0-692-77769-5

First Edition: October 2016

Published and printed in the United States of America.

To my wife, Mena, and my daughter, Kelli;
my world.

"It's not when you had your last drink that counts..."

Contents

Contents - continued

The Black
SHEEP

Foreword

Tom "Running Man" McGrath is truly one of the most amazing, generous, compassionate, caring, and dedicated people I have ever known. He has a heart as big as all the outdoors and that's where you'll usually find him, running hundreds of thousands of miles to raise money for children with disabilities, Hospice care centers, and families needing help to pay medical expenses for cancer treatment. The list goes on and on. His desire to help others is quite simply, boundless.

We at Achilles Kids, a running-walking-rolling program for children with disabilities, are so blessed to have had Tom's support the past three years. Each year Tom runs a mind boggling "Six Marathons in Six Days for Achilles Kids," and the money we have raised through his marathons have provided running shoes to more than 12,000 children with disabilities. For many of our kids, these are the first pair of brand new sneakers they have ever received. We are, and will always be, truly grateful for his support and in awe of the depth of his compassion for those in need.

Karen Lewis
Achilles Kids

Timeline

1950 Born in Ederney, Northern Ireland
.
.
.

1961 Left Home for "The Brothers of Charity"
1966 St. Michael's; Fermanagh Super Bowl of Gaelic Football
1968 St. Joseph's; Started boxing club
1969 Visited New York to play Gaelic Football; Started running
1970 U21 All Ireland Final (Gaelic Football)
1971 U21 All Ireland Final (Gaelic Football)
1974 Opened first bar in NYC
1975 World Tour of Gaelic Football
1977 Trans-American Run
1978 Started drinking regularly
.

1984 Explored the dark side as a blackjack dealer; NYRR 100
     Miler (3rd Place) NYRR 6 Day Run
1988 First 1,000 mile race
1989 First 1,000 mile solo run around Central Park Reservoir
1991 Opened "Tom McGrath's"
     Alcohol abuse became serious
1996 Chosen as a torch bearer for the Olympic Games
.
.
.

2010 DWI and near death consequences
2011 Six Counties Run in Northern Ireland
2012 250 mile run to Annapolis, MD for Commodore John Barry
2016 Clean and at the helm of "The Black Sheep on 38th and
     Third

1

Who Is This Guy?

All I want is for somebody to tell me who I am, to put the parts together and make sense of it all. I've run for miles and miles, days, weeks, 300 miles at a time, 1,000 miles, and even across the country. I've totaled over 200,000 miles in my life for charity, alone. I've also owned over 10 bars in New York City, one of the most competitive places in the world for three decades running. I just finished a 12-hour race to ring in this, yet another new year. I'm 66 years old and I'm one of the fittest bar owners you're likely to meet but, some might think, one of the unfittest.

I come from one of the poorest backgrounds you can imagine, where people's lives haven't changed much over hundreds of years. Yet, I've been blessed with seeing some of the craziest sights any person could ever dream up. I've landed myself in situations that I should never have been in and never should have gotten out of. How can you have the discipline and determination, the "steel in the concrete" to push yourself to keep running and manage a business and not have the will power to say "no," I'll not have another drink?

I am, or at least was, an alcoholic and a mighty one at that. It took me an enormous amount of time to be able to say that. Alcoholism is a disease. Or is it? Bottom line, it eats the human's insides until death.

1

Only if the brain can mature to the point it understands it is killing itself, can a person be saved. I didn't stop till my eyes turned yellow. My whole body turned yellow. When the doctor tells you, "you have a week to live. You created your own deathbed," or "the next fall could be your last fall," perhaps you'll listen, or maybe, you won't. We all fall. We know that. But, what if you are the one knocking yourself down?

History tells us St. Patrick was buried without a jaw and missing teeth. Honestly, many times I must have thought that I was St. Patrick himself, my jaw broken, teeth missing, but the vodka was still in front of me. I've had nearly every bone above my waist broken at least once. I've cleared my own bar out in a drunken rage on the biggest day of the year, St. Patrick's. If there is one thing I know about myself it's that I don't do anything half-assed. If I do it, I go all the way and that includes drinking.

Emigrating from Ireland is a unique experience. If you've done it, you know what I'm talking about. You step off of one planet and land on another. For us in the North, we left a war zone and came to the land of boundless opportunity. So, why would you ever have a care in the world? "Because you're Irish," they tell me, as if that explains everything, but being Irish didn't make me an alcoholic. I did that, and I did that in America, not in Ireland. But why? How? No one in my family drank.

I love to run. I love to listen to my body hum along the road, the heart, the lungs, the arms and legs, all like a one-man band. I love the feel of the road beneath me and I can feel the body inhaling peace deep into my soul. When I run, I don't drink and the opposite is true as well. Nobody actually goes out there to run for five hours for their health. They may say so, but there is more to that. For me, I couldn't stop and I didn't want to stop. I would keep running till there was nowhere left to run, literally. I ran clear across this continent from one ocean to the other. You have to be out of your skull to do runs like that. "Did you ever feel like quitting?" they asked me. "Every five minutes" was my answer. I swore every time I finished a monstrous multi-day run, "never again. That's it." I said "never again" thousands of times, just as many

2

times after a run as after destroying my body with alcohol. "Never again, never again that."

I love people. I love talking to people. I love my family, but I've hurt them all, tremendously.

Temptation is only a word they say, floating through the air, but it's everywhere. "How can you own a bar?" they say. I tell them every morning I say "hello" to all my whiskey bottles. They are my friends, but also my enemies. Whiskey demands immediate respect. No respect, no mercy. It will crush the body like a bulldozer.

Ultrarunning is the same. You must respect the course ahead of you and respect your body—and therein lies the crux; how can the mind justify destroying the body? I did, in so many ways. Perhaps, you do too.

Temptation is defined in the self, to be handled with extreme caution, head-on or disaster can strike. We all slip on the road we're on, but ultimately, if balance is to be found, you alone are responsible. I can't tell you how to live. I can only tell you how I have. If God could turn back my clock, there would be massive changes.

2

Fitness In The Black Sheep

The human mind is an extremely curious body part. As a bar owner, selling a "legalized drug" in moderation, a lot of mysteries develop and unfold. The feelings, attitudes, and moods created by alcohol are truly amazing. One that keeps coming around is about my fitness. "You must be the fittest bar owner in New York," they say. "I have to go to the gym with you." "I will run you around the block." These are only a few of the comments I get almost on a daily basis, when I come from the gym.

I work out twice a day, every day. "If you were an ice cream cone, you would lick yourself," one customer told me. He meant well. I smiled at the pack of Marlboro in his top pocket and the bottle of Bud in his hand. That is what I call "good envy." There is also a guilt that comes over them in regards to my training, "look at him, there, eating an apple and I'm over here guzzling a bottle." When customers start talking about running and joining the gym, I know that 99 out of 100 times, it won't happen. The whiskey is talking. It's good at making you make promises, that the alcohol, itself, will keep you from achieving. Their intentions are great, but their willpower is zero. "I don't have time for the gym," I hear all too often. "You have to make time," I say. Money doesn't trump wealth. "Your health is your wealth" as the old saying goes. It's hard to spend money in a pine box. The simple fact is, the fitter your are, the harder you can work.

Most people are escaping work when they come to my bar. One guy came in and said, "I have to come here. This is my cool escape bar." It helped with the pressure riding him, he said. Another happy tourist called my bar "an oasis in a zoo." He had come back for a second day, while he was waiting to go to a concert. Bars can become a way of life and changing lifestyles for most can be harder than restarting a bad marriage. Instead of facing it, they wear the ring of whiskey till death do they part.

I run on the road for an hour and a half each day. I start at my bar and make my way south into The Village. I pass a church and turn towards the river. I hit another church there and head back west, stopping in Tompkins Square Park. I come back up north on Broadway and head right through the busiest parts of the city, Herald Square and Times Square. People are mystified by that, but I have my reasons.

If I plan to do a long four to five hour run, I head straight to the Hudson River and run up to the George Washington Bridge, before making my way back down. I do this more and more often leading up to a big run. If I do a short run, I run south as usual, but cut the route short on the west side and just head north back to my bar. That is an hour.

When it snows so heavy you can't run on the street, I do steps in Grand Central, thousands of them. I start at the bottom with the 7 train and run all the way up to street side, right on Third Avenue. I repeat that four to five times. People always look at you strange riding the escalator. They cut their eyes at the guy in the orange tank top and bright shorts. "That's me, people. I run. And you know why? Not just to stay healthy, but to keep my grit."

Grit is something that is dying in cultures all over the world. It is the persistence to see something through, despite adversity. The more adversity you overcome, the more grit you have and the stronger the chance that you will be successful, no matter what you attempt. A grit of sand can make a pearl. Embrace the adversity and cultivate the willpower in you to go out no matter what the externals are in your life. Run when it's cold and run faster when it's hot. Focus more when you are tired and sweat more when you want to take a nap.

Every day I hit the gym and when I do, I say hello to all the machines. They are my friends. I start off with 300 sit ups, two sets of 150. Next, I hit the upper body with presses, butterflies, and rope work. I burn the muscle, then I roll it. I always bring a roller with me. It is a piece of hardened foam with ripply edges and you roll your muscles on it to relieve built up tension. They often call me "the roller man." That's okay with me. I know how I must look, coming in with a roller in one hand and a cup of coffee in the other. I do the legs last, pressing 200 to 300 times, depending on the day. Every day, I do my lower back, holding a 25-pound weight.

Tom training in the streets of New York City

When I was a member of the NY Racquet Club, I would run in the steam room. That was a great workout. It was all fine until the damn

6

towel boy turned me in. I had to grab him up by the neck and give him the what for, which is what the front office then gave me. They threatened to toss me. At Jack LaLanne's Gym, I ran so long on the treadmill, that huge lines would form. Let's just say I was not so popular, there. One day, it broke. They blamed me. They said I ran it to death. Eventually, I built my own steam room at home and run in it several times a week.

My bathtub is my second gym. I grab the faucet with my feet and do 100 sit ups right out of the water and add 50 to 60 dips on to that, just quiet enough that the wife doesn't hear.

Oh yes, I used to run with garbage bags and I would run with 80 pound weights, but that's not what's important. It's the grit. The fact that you do it, every day. You don't excuse yourself out of it. That builds a grit inside you that will see you through almost anything, even a deathbed of alcohol.

A man's greatest strength doesn't always nullify his deepest weakness. There were too many nights, when customers would stare at me, the angry intoxicated animal in the corner, and never believe I was a world champion.

3

The Bridge

I was in a dark tunnel that seemed to go on forever. It took over 3,000 miles for me to get there, but the ultimate goal and the world record was on the other side. When the sky opened up above me and I came out of that tunnel, there stood the Golden Gate Bridge. Fifty-three days before, I left New York, on foot. It was 1977 and I was on top of the world. "Why run against the wind, east to west, from New York to San Fran?" reporters asked. That was the logical way to go and the way most runners did it, but I always go my own way. I'm a black sheep.

All that was left was to cross that bridge. The world record was right in my pocket. Massive speakers were set up on the sides, "Congratulations Tom McGrath. Welcome to San Francisco." That message meant more to me, personally, than many know. In so many ways, it was like my life. There is more to being an Irish emigrant than people see on the surface, more to being Catholic, when the rent collectors are Protestant, and more to the stigma of an old Irish bar fighter than most books will tell you. Coming out of the war-torn North and landing in America to begin with was the longest tunnel of my life.

To run across that Golden Gate Bridge was nothing, physically. What are 2 miles out of thousands? Mentally, it was much longer than that. The truth was that I had been to San Francisco before. In fact, I was kicked out and told never to come back.

It was 1972. I was working as a bartender on the upper west side of Manhattan. A man comes to me and says, "How'd you like to go to California?" I said that would be great. He had a ticket and couldn't go. It was a free ride, so I took it. I quit my job and headed out with my friend Paddy. We got there and saw the sights. Needless to say, we wound up in a bar with another friend, Colum Healy. He was from Dublin and Paddy and I were from the North. The bar was full of girls at noon on a Sunday, if you can imagine that. Paddy and Colum got into it over politics and blows flew. I got between them and took them outside, where the cops were waiting for us. I said there was no problem and that they were just arguing about football. Never mention anything about politics. It could only get you into more trouble.

Back in the bar. They started at it again and we were kicked out once more. This time, they arrested all three of us. They locked us up, each in our own cell. Well, Paddy was a singer and he started in with an old Irish song, "the judge said, 'stand up lad.'" Soon, we all joined in.

It was a miserable place. You had no idea what kind of criminal was next to you. In my cell, a man came in wearing prison stripes. I was lying on a bench and he sat on me legs. I jumped up and socked him square in the jaw. "You sit down there," I said to him. You had to be tough. I wasn't about to get pushed around in there. One of the jailers came up to the bars and pointed to me. I went over to him. "You know we got cameras, don't ya?" He then told me if I was gonna hit someone, not to leave any marks.

The next morning, they brought all three of us to the judge. Apparently, we had become known as the three Irishmen in lockup. The judge called Paddy first, "Ten years' hard labor for singing in jail." Shock stunned all three of us silent. "You, Mr. McGrath, five years for trying to sing in jail." Jokes sometimes have a jolt to them before you get a hold of it. I just heard ten years, then five years and hard labor. He then pounded on his desk with that gavel and pointed it at us. He told us to get out of San Francisco and to never come back, ever.

First thing we did, when we got out was to book tickets back to New York. While I waited for the plane, we drove over to San Quentin to take a look at that prison. So, we went from one prison to another. The guard there says, "what you wanna see in here?" He didn't let us in and we turned around to go back and find some sleep. Wouldn't you know it, blue lights came up behind us. I pulled over, driving Colum's car. Turned out, our friend Colum had expired plates. The officer asked to see me license. At that time, I had a Northern Ireland driver's license, which was written in pen. Mine had expired in '71, but I took a marker, not a good match apparently, and changed that one to a four, giving myself an extra three years. He saw it right off, "you did this yourself." Silent again.

Back in the same jail we had just left, the sergeant looked mystified, "McGrath," he said, "what the hell are you doing back here?" I told him the bit and that I had a ticket to go back to New York. He actually checked with the airlines to make sure that I was leaving the city. He held me till time to get the flight, then let me free.

Five years later, it did cross my mind that they might be there at the bridge as I was running in, but instead there were those incredible words, "welcome to San Francisco." I had run across the new world on my own two legs and set a new World Record at that. It was a special night in that magical city and one I'll never forget.

That night I looked back across the land I'd crossed and wondered how in the world I'd gotten to where I was. Indeed, I had a second chance at things. The journey across the ocean from my home in Ireland was even tougher. How did I get out? Why me? I left everything that was comfortable; friends, loved ones, and the familiar rolling hills of my youth. Then, of course, there was the hardship, the hunger, the persecution. The deserts of America that I'd crossed were so different than the land I'd grown up on, but they had one thing in common. They were both barren.

Crossing the Golden Gate Bridge, setting the World Record

4

Fermanagh

Potatoes grow in the worst dirt. They are tough, hardy, and are one of nature's perfect foods. You can survive on potatoes alone. I know, cause we did. My father would come in, spread them out on the concrete yard outside our home. He'd sprinkle salt over them and give us all a cup of milk. You dip them in the milk and you have yourself a meal. To this day, I eat my potatoes the same way.

The Potato Famine is an English term. We never called it that, because it had nothing to do with the lumbar, the type of potato that was hit with the blight. It was about being marginalized, discriminated against, and treated like second class human beings. We call it "the great famine" or "the hunger." We didn't starve. We were starved. We were owned and the owners weren't even around. When things got bad enough and they did come, they would stay up in a town and make the farmers come to them to pay what they owed. Many Irish died that way, too weak to walk. There are stones that still litter Ireland today, where women, children, and husbands fell to the Earth, never to walk again, not because there wasn't enough food, but because someone wanted more for themselves or to punish us for our religion.

Fermanagh is up near the top of Ireland, set back in the rolling hills and farms, and that is where I came into this world. I was born legs kicking. That's what we all do, really. We are born running with our wee legs going as fast as they can. There were 11 of us kids, eight being boys. Like a step of stairs, each year another boy was born. That's a lot of mouths to feed with very little food and limited clothing. I learned to eat fast. Otherwise, you'd go hungry. I would put a spoonful in my hand, where nobody could see it. That way, I always had an extra bite. First up in the morning, got the food and the best of whatever clothes were there. I remember vividly, in the school yard, watching, with my mouth watering, the other kids eating a big sandwich. I wanted a bite of that so badly. In hindsight, that taught us so much, especially, the power of the family. The power of love. On the way home from school, we would pick berries off the trees and rob whatever orchards there were, stealing carrots or turnips out of the ground. That was food to us, cooked or uncooked. Just wipe off the dirt and right into the stomach she goes. I would pick blackberries for my mother to make homemade jam. Very simple. Crush the berries, add sugar, and we had a jam party. A jam sandwich was a big meal. Butter did not exist in our family budget.

At night, we would all gather around the hearth fire. Basically, it was a fire on the floor and we'd go through the same routine, every night. My mother was very religious. Two of my siblings became clergy and my mother wanted the same for me. We would kneel down, every evening, and pray for everybody, including our neighbors. Then, we said the Rosary and that would last an hour and a half. I used to avoid it as much as possible. I wanted to be active. Afterward, we would all have corn flakes or cocoa drink. I would crush my corn flakes into a bowl. You get more in that way. I still eat my corn flakes the same way. That was our supper. When we were done eating, we'd say, "mum, it's time to go to bed." We'd ship her off upstairs and then we'd move the furniture to the side. We'd tie paper up with a string and make a ball out of it. We'd play soccer in the living room with the two doors as goal posts. The two girls, Anne and Geraldine, were the goalies and we boys would beat each other up on the playing field. Mother would hear the racket, but by the time she made it downstairs to the Irish Super Bowl, all the players were sitting, "mum, are you dreaming again?"

Our farm was barren. A half-ass bog claimed part of it and the rest was not good for much. We'd go in there to get turf. In Ireland, this is peat, taken from a bog, dried, and used like wood. We'd lumber up over the hills, pulling that stuff back home. Those days were hard work. When we didn't have enough turf, being in short supply of trees on our own land, we'd skip over to our neighbor's land and cut some of their wood and beat a path back with it. We all need water, but in Ireland, water is anything but scarce. There are tons of it everywhere—30% of Fermanagh is rivers and lakes. In my real young days, we had to go to a "wee well" and carry home buckets of water, because the Protestant-run government said they couldn't run the water up the hill to our place. The well was located right next to a stream, but honestly, I think we were not drinking spring water. Nevertheless, it tasted good. We were also one of the few families that didn't have electricity.

Living on a barren farm was difficult. In my younger days, we had no machinery. Everything was done by hand, which I tried to avoid, but there was no escape. You stayed quiet and did your job. We cut the hay for the scant amount of cattle we had. We did that with a scythe and cut the turf with a spade. I would get terrible headaches in the hay fields, so I hated that, but not as much as spreading the cow dung. We all tried to get out of that duty. Headaches weren't an excuse. In truth, there were no excuses. You did it.

When the animals gave birth, it was a big celebration, but we didn't have anything fancy; no champagne, no wine, no whiskey. As a child, I witnessed the births of calves, pigs, puppies, chickens, and goats, to name a few. What a unique experience, but what an ugly sight. If a cow had a stillborn calf, we would try to fool her by putting her cleanings on an active calf. It never worked. "That's not my blood. You don't fool me," she seemed to say as she stared at us. Growing up on a farm gives you a special love for nature and its products: the animals, the trees, the flowers, the rivers and the lakes. They are all so, so beautiful.

The biggest prize, besides food, was getting your own pet animal. If they ever got sick or died, you'd cry like the world had ended. I had my own pet lamb, puppy, and goat. They were the life within our lives and got more hugs than we ever got. Working on a farm has to be the healthiest life on the planet. We ate the food from the Earth. We breathed clean fresh air and did physical work all day long. It was extremely important to the development of the mind and the body, teaching us to respect nature and accept the acts of God, whether we believed them to be good or bad.

The McGrath brothers: top left, Brendan, Sean, and Leonard. Bottom left, Tom and Cairan

As a child, I saw first-hand how decent, loving, and compassionate the Irish farmers were. They all banded together when there was a problem. It didn't matter which religion you were, Catholic or Protestant. If the cattle got stuck in the river or a bog, help arrived immediately. When threshing the corn, all joined in. If food was needed, it was shared and last of all, when my mum was giving birth, the neighbors were there to lend "a helping hand."

For quite a few summers, I was sent to my grandfather's house and cousins' homes. Honestly, looking back on it, I was one less mouth to feed. My grandfather was blind and all day long I'd tickle his nose with a feather. First, he thought it was a fly, but then he'd swing the stick at me. He always missed the target. All the time I was there, all I ever ate was boiled eggs and homemade bread.

I remember my mother making shorts out of the flour pack after she was finished making the bread, which was always devoured before it could ever get cold. We'd churn the milk to make butter, but we were never too successful. Every egg was important, but often, I'd sneak into the hen house like a fox and eat about seven raw eggs. Tough job, that. You crack the egg, close your eyes and swallow it as fast as possible. God gave me a full head of hair to this day, that's for sure, but I think all the eggs and milk had a helping hand. When we were done milking the cow, I used to drink it warm, straight out of the bucket. That milk was nice and foamy, but I didn't care for it warm like that. Either way, I had to satisfy the appetite, but the rest of my brothers wouldn't go near that bucket. Nothing in a poor family ever, ever goes to waste.

My mother did her utmost to keep us up to standard as far as hygiene was concerned. That was tough on a muddy, wet farm. Every week, at least once or twice, we would line up for a bath. What a battle that was, jumping into a big aluminum bath pan, fists and legs flying. Control was the biggest problem, but we got our baths. At bath time, it was the custom to get the hair washed with soap and then my mother gave us a little extra stuff to make sure the animals hadn't given us any unwelcome visitors. She did an excellent job in such primitive circumstances. Washing machines were unheard of, so the clothes were scrubbed on a good old "washboard," then put on the hedge or a clothes line. The wind always did the job of drying.

I worked on a neighbor's farm for 10 shillings a week. Back then, that was a dollar a week. Those were 10 hour days, six days a week, because mum and dad needed the money for us to survive. Inside bathrooms were a major luxury and having no plumbing, no running water, we had the pleasure of using the famous "outhouse." I remember in the dark of night, in the howling wind and lashing rain, going out to that toilet, absolutely terrified. We were lucky to have a flashlight for guidance. Fortunately for us kids, our poor father had the honor of keeping it clean. The only consolation we had was that we were not alone. A high percentage of Ireland was in the same boat and look what a nation we became, gaining so much respect all around the world.

Birthplace

My father was a tough, hard working, simple man. He didn't express his opinion much, but we respected him. He taught me what it is to work hard and my mother showed me the power of believing in something. We fought to stay on our land. It was ours. I can't tell you what that means to an Irishman. When your land has been taken away and you become a prisoner in your own fields, you learn to respect every bit of dirt you have when you get it back.

5

The Brothers

Looking back on school in Ireland, I can only classify it as, "the good ole days." We started off in the "low infants" class, moved to "high infants" class, and then to primary school. However, we did have to fight to be Catholic, every day. Protestant England was very much at odds with Catholic Ireland and we weren't about to give an inch of our freedom away, especially when it came to God. Walking to school and back, fights would break out with non-Catholics. They weren't always the ones starting it, neither. "Put them through the hedge," we'd say.

At age 11, one moved to either secondary school, paid for by the government, or if you passed a special exam, one moved to what in Ireland is called "college." In the U.S., it's called high school. Back then in the '50s and '60s, placement in different schools may have created a lot of inferior feelings for those that failed the exam, of which I was one, but I still qualified as a physical education teacher later in life.

That was the system. Catholics went to their own school. Protestants went to theirs, and in my opinion, that may have bred discrimination between both religions. We are just visiting this Earth. Every day is another day in "paradise," and there is no place for discrimination, whatsoever. Having failed my exam called "11 plus," I had no choice but to attend a public secondary school, what is called junior high school in the U.S. It was called St. Mary's. It was a brand new school and not just for me. It was literally, the first year of the school. I was totally flabbergasted when I saw the gym. My eyes almost fell out and my heart pounded with such excitement. A real gym. Not a bar with lumber planks as beams and rocks as weights on a concrete floor. After my first class, I knew I wanted to be a gym teacher and fulfilled that beautiful dream 10 years later.

During that year, a member of "The Brothers of Charity" came looking for recruits to join the Order and lo and behold, I thought I had at least a temporary vocation. The Brother spoke at our gym and was so striking. They were like priests except they didn't say Mass. He was from the South and impressed me like no one ever had. I decided I wanted to be one of these "Brothers" and I had my mother's blessing. My older brother, Sean, and sister, Bernadette, were both in the clergy, so it seemed to be a perfect Catholic family in my parents' eyes, who were very religious, hard working people and even though we had nothing to give, they bred the gift of giving into our blood. Worldly goods aside, we could always lend a hand to the weary, the sick, and those who needed help. It's so easy to be nice.

Sometimes we can't see the nose on our own face. My brothers and sisters knew me much better than I knew myself. "You were always running, everywhere," my sister Anne tells me, "you were always moving. You had some place to be, something to do." I've come to realize, for some, the world just isn't big enough for the energy we were born with. In my 20/20 glasses of hindsight, it was in my mother's eyes all along. Like Moma Jode, who knows she can't keep Tom any longer, my mother had to let me go.

In September, 1961, at 11 years old, I left home for the first time on a 250-mile journey down to Cork City in the South, all by myself. Imagine your child, now, doing such a thing. My first journey into the "real world" had me dressed in short pants, a long jacket, a little suitcase, two slices of bread and jam wrapped in newspaper in my pocket, and a healthy smile telling the whole world, "here comes Tom." What a journey, never to be forgotten. After boarding the train in Omagh and saying goodbye to mum and dad, the journey took a turn for the worse. On the train was another boy, 13 years old, who was running up and down the train, so I joined the hide and seek game. About 20 miles outside of Dublin, my playmate informed me that he was going to jump off the train. To my horror and disbelief, he pulled the stop chain, waited till the train almost stopped, and jumped off right in front of my eyes. Immediately, I was surrounded by the crew and blamed for everything. They said, "you pulled the chain." I said, "no I did not. It was the other boy." Of course, they came back with, "what boy? Where is he? Who is he?" These questions they fired at me, then brought me to the front of the train and delivered me to the police.

The police station in Dublin wasn't the welcome I was looking for, but I let them know that my mother told me to eat my sandwich when I got there, and they let me do so. Can you believe they just let me go to walk alone in the middle of Dublin? Imagine that. I hardly had a hair on my chest and they sent me out into the streets. I remember walking right passed Nelson's Pillar.

Up went Nelson in old Dublin
Up went Nelson in old Dublin
All along O'Connell Street
The stones and rubble flew
As up went Nelson and the pillar, too

After leaving my detention with GARDA (Irish Police), I walked from the North side of Dublin to the South side and boarded a train to Cork City. Cork City is located at the very South of Ireland, about 250 miles from my home. My first four hours into the real world by myself at 11 years old were extremely hectic and very exciting. Not too many children get arrested for questioning on their first journey of life.

My second four hours on the train were peaceful, but lonely. After all, I had just said goodbye to my parents and whole family, not knowing what to expect in the jungle of life outside Fermanagh. That was the most emotional trip of my life, having thoughts of joining the clergy or not. I was trying to imitate my brother, Sean, who was studying for the priesthood. That was known as "a mother's vocation." I was trying to please her. I really didn't know anything about me, but I soon found out. In this world it is every man for himself.

God helps those who help themselves. Upon reaching Cork City, I was driven to a college, St. Declan's, out in the country surrounded by beautiful scenery, rolling hills, valleys, and lakes. It seemed the perfect place to cultivate the baby inkling of devoting my celibate life to helping others. It was my first time to see a college, to see 80 students line up, to see religious Brothers show their authority.

The Brothers were a strict bunch. Rules and regulations were all over the place. Bedtime was 10. We were up at 5:30 a.m. for Mass, every day, then meals, then work. Clean the house spotless. Class all day and study for three hours at night. I missed my family so much, the second night there, I cried my eyes out. It seemed like I went from an innocent farm life to a jail. I was not used to orders or commands. I had never really heard complete silence. I never thought I'd sleep next to 79 other boys. I wanted to say, but I couldn't "I want to go home." Yet, the urge to be a Brother was still a seed in my gut, and it soon grew. Still, I always visited home on Christmas, Easter, and during the summer.

They were a physical bunch and that was alright with me. They had team sports. I loved it. Basketball. Ping Pong, when it was raining and Gaelic Football. Vincent Walsh, my loyal pal, would stand there all day as my goalie, while I peppered him with balls.

Needless to say, I got in some scuffs. I'd stand back, push my chest out and let any of them take a whack at me. Almost on a daily basis, I had to defend my Irish heritage. Being from the North, I was regarded as a foreigner, an Englishman, to which I took great offense. I responded with my fists most of the time and as a result, I was punished often, like Steve McQueen in *The Great Escape*. All eyes were on me as I was called in. Punishment came in various forms. I was made to clean the toilets, clean the church, and always placed on the front seat of every class. The front seat was the biggest torture, because there wasn't anybody in front of me to poke. I was under supervision all of the time. I really think the Brothers knew that my vocation was fading rapidly. So, after four years, I was given an option, join the novitiate, take my first vows, or leave. It broke my mother's heart, but I had to say no. That wasn't for me.

Discipline and willpower are like the kings and queens of the spirit, together, they make power. Those four years carried my body and soul through all of my ultramarathons and ultimately, saved my life. They helped me climb out of the tomb of alcohol abuse. Those four years were full of every emotion that life breeds in young souls. I thank the Brothers of Charity for the time I spent with them.

The McGrath children: top left, Leonard, Sean, Anthony, Colum, Brendan. Bottom left, Anne, Maurice, Cairan, Tom, Geraldine

6

The Mighty McGraths

If basketball, soccer, and American Football were to have a baby, it would be Gaelic Football. You play on a pitch, similar to soccer, but above the net, you have goal posts like the NFL. You can bounce the ball, but not twice in a row. Sound familiar? You can catch the ball and kick the ball on the ground, but there are rules. You have to chip the ball, kick it from the ground to your hands, and you can punch the ball to other players. You can lower your shoulder in Gaelic Football and put the boom on someone. It's hard stuff. No helmets, no pads. You bounce the ball and run and kick. I broke some bones, but went all the way to the Fermanagh Senior Championship by the time I was 16.

It's Ireland's national sport and it's completely amateur. There are no professional teams. That keeps it gritty. Gaelic Football or Irish Football has been around in many forms for centuries and is the heart of old Ireland's soul. It is the most attended sport in Ireland with up to 80,000 showing up for real big matches. The heroes of the pitch are still remembered today, Dan O'Keeffe, Mikey Sheehy, Tommy Langan, and of course, Michael Hogan.

Hogan was on a train bound for Croke Park, Dublin, when he and some players got into a scuffle with some British Lincolnshire soldiers. They managed to throw the soldiers from the train. The next day, at a match at Croke Stadium, British soldiers entered, guns in hand, cocked and loaded, and proceeded to open fire on everyone in the stadium. Fourteen people were killed and over 60 injured, including spectators. Hogan was on the pitch, shot, and dying. A lad named Tom Ryan, from Wexford, ran onto the field and knelt beside Hogan, praying for his life. Wee Tom Ryan was shot and killed as he prayed there and died with his football hero in the middle of the pitch. This was Bloody Sunday, November 21, 1920.

There are too many massacres to go into, but you should know there was a September 11th long before the one we know of. In 2002, Oliver Cromwell was voted in a BBC poll as one of the 10 greatest Brits of all time. This same Cromwell, on September 11, 1649, razed the city of Drogheda, killing over 3,500 Irish men, women, and children. He made no distinction between soldiers and citizens and particularly targeted the Churches. He called it "the vengeance of God," and labeled Irish Catholics as "barbarous wretches." If your family escaped that, you wouldn't easily forget it.

They could never stop us from playing football. In fact, Gaelic Football became more organized and the counties are represented in a super bowl match each year. I've played in it, but it may not have been my toughest match.

Growing up on a farm in Fermanagh with seven other brothers was a very exciting and healthy lifestyle. With no TV, we had physical activity and hard work. That was the only lifestyle we knew. At a very young age playing cowboys and Indians was major in developing the motor skills which we needed later for the contact sports, like Gaelic Football, which became my life. I thought about it morning, noon, and night. I scored goals in my sleep.

In Fermanagh, we didn't have a proper pitch, so we made our own on our farm. All my brothers played and we became known for one skill above all others, being tough. If you beat us, you'd remember it, cause you'd be sore as the dickens. We formed our own team and we were called the "Mighty McGraths." In those early days, I wasn't the biggest, but I played, as they say, with a chip on my shoulder. Growing up in the country is similar all over the world. There are two ways to separate yourself and prove you aren't a kid anymore. That is by drinking more than they can and being tougher than they are. We didn't drink, so we were tough as nails.

The Mighty McGraths

In my teens, some Sundays, I played three games, one after another. For at least four years, I never had a Sunday without football. I'll never forget some of my earliest memories of watching the footballers getting "togged out." In Ireland this is what we call *putting all their gear on.* I can see them, now, behind the trees getting ready to do battle, no bathrooms, no showers, no warm ups, just hit the field and belt the hell out of each other for an hour. I remember often thinking, "I am better than them," and the four years at St. Declan's College with "The Brothers" gave me the opportunity to prove it. I was the youngest one there and the only one from the North of Ireland. I was the British guy, they said. I played at all levels and represented Fermanagh for years. The highlight of my football career was playing for Fermanagh in two, under 21, All Ireland Finals. I took the pitch in that game in '70 and '71.

My style was explosiveness. At 5-foot-8, I wasn't going to win many balls in the air, so I developed a strategy. Most big guys slam into each other going up for balls. Usually, they never get it. It comes plopping down to the ground around them and then there is a mad scramble. I developed the art of not jumping, but guessing just when and where the ball would come off those brutes. When I got it, I made a straight line for the goal, no weaving or fancy footwork, just a bullet towards that net.

After leaving St. Declan's, in Cork, I was 16, strong and determined, without restrictions or commands. I had to accept my freedom, again; a whole new kind of life. After telling my mother, that I was not returning to "The Brother's of Charity," she was extremely disappointed.

"What are you going to do with your life, now?"

"Construction," I said, showing her an ad in the Irish News. Never doubt the love of a mother and the power they hold. She went down to St. Michael's, a prestigious academic sports school, met with the president, Father McElroy, and got me accepted.

Coming from a family, poorer than poor, it was a tremendous honor to attend that school. Gaelic Football was the predominant sport; my delight, my joy, and my life. After three weeks, I entered a 2-mile race on the school's sports day.

The race was around a cow field with holes, weeds, and manure. That was the track. The race knackered me to no end. Packets Maguire won the race, leaving me in the dust, but I came in second. I was on the athletic map and the whole school seemed to know my name. It was vital to me to blend in.

There was a Protestant girl's school just blocks away and we all walked together. We had 20/20 vision on those walks. My sheltered life from female company had to be adjusted, to say the least. At 16, I entered another new world of curiosity. "How did the other half live?" The morning and evening walks helped set things in motion. Some of the students drove their own cars to school. I came with 40 others on a bus, boys and girls all together. Every day on those buses was a new day full of fun and laughter. "Fun trips" we called them, because there we were, boys, girls, Catholics and Protestants, side by side, no discrimination.

At St. Michael's, I somehow climbed the ladder of popularity relatively quick. It's still a mystery to me, but after my first year, I was elected prefect and voted house captain. That meant I had to be a model student and curtail my wild streak. Only 6 months after receiving those honors, I was caught downtown playing hooky with Phil Sheridan and stripped of all my badges.

My curiosity was just too strong for such possibilities.

I passed my exams at 18 and was back in limbo. What was I going to do with the life I'd been given? The clergy vocation and following in my brother Sean's footsteps had evaporated and I wasn't keen on working construction. The one thing that stuck with me was the feeling of that first gym. It's so easy for many of us to take something like a gym for granted, but to me, it was a kind of heaven, where the body could float into all kinds of positions. To me, it was a mystical place. It was a place where one could show the power and strength of this unique, God given machine, the human body.

So, I decided I wanted all of those and to pass them down until the end of time. Financial matters were not a priority. Your health is indeed your wealth. I've never lost that mantra. I wanted to be a physical education teacher. Having made the decision against the advice of some other teachers, who were concerned about money, I applied to colleges in Belfast and England.

In October of '68, off to St. Joseph's in Belfast I went with 6 buddies from St. Michael's. There were 60 applicants for 12 positions as PE teachers and my ability and skills earned a position as one of the 12. Studying PE meant being involved in a host of sports and gymnastics.

Now my dream of exercise was coming to fruition and I loved every second of it. I was a happy man. Back then, being a qualified teacher was a very respectable job. I remember well all the farmers after Sunday Mass, addressing me as sir, to which I answered "Tom is my name. Forget the sir."

St. Joseph's was a college under the direction of Queen's University as my certificate states. My first year as a resident, to a certain degree, reminded me of the four years in Cork. Supervision was a lot less, however. Freedom was a nice bonus to have at that age in life. Our first year there was a little wild and we were regarded as "The Fermanagh Bunch," responsible for any misconduct, whatsoever. Nine months later two of the so called "bunch" were diplomatically asked to leave for undisclosed reasons, but the rest remained in their allotted training time. While I was there, I did not drink and a lot of the time, I was the designated driver. Looking back, it was my first real introduction to alcohol abuse. Being a non-drinker, I thought it was strange, but it never entered my head that so many people were on a path of destruction.

Years later, unfortunately, I walked every inch of that path and heard about other fellow students doing the same. Where once, we boys attended wakes of strangers to get a bit of food, I went to way too many as an adult, of bar owners that had succumbed to alcohol abuse.

Jim McKeever was head of the PE Department. He was a former football star and had earned the name "Gentleman Jim." He was a heck of a man. We had periodic six-part exams in each year, including gymnastics and coordination drills. There was a big farmer boy on our team. He must have been about 6-foot-4 and 250 pounds of muscle. He fell off everything, ropes, the pommel horse, you name it. He nearly broke the parallel bars. My job was to evaluate him. Scores went from one to 10. I gave him a nine, the best, and got a call into McKeever's office. "Mr. McKeever," I told him, "you tell him he failed. I wanna live."

I loved to listen to Muhammad Ali fight on the transistor radio as a kid. My dad was a quiet, humble man, but he loved boxing. Sitting there with him, we could both picture Ali floating and stinging. With eight brothers in a confined space, boxing will be on the menu. We strung up a make shift boxing bag in the barn made from hay and potato sacks. We'd fill it up with rags and punch it to pieces. Kept us from pummeling each other too much. I got an early start in the defense department. Sometimes our mother would hide the gloves, cause soon enough it would turn into a melee. We were tough.

So, at St. Joseph's Training College, I did something completely off the college hierarchy's radar, I started a boxing club. I organized a fight with Queens University, a big time school. It would be like William and Mary taking on Alabama in football. They still talk about it. The British Army had taken control of St. Joseph's during "The Troubles," so there were tanks all around. The only problem was we didn't have a ring. Something had to be done, so I made a deal with the soldiers. I told them we were going to have a fight, a great one, the little guy beating up the big guy. They gave us the ring and came to see the fight. Front row. We won. The wee boys hammered the big boys, not once, but twice.

Marty McGrath

Gaelic Football, actually, brought me to America on June 16, 1969, to play in New York. Then, I had the privilege of playing for New York in March of '75 on a world tour, which included playing in Hawaii,

Australia and New Zealand. In New York, we would play up in the Bronx. Gaelic Park sits just south of Van Cortland Park and is the largest Gaelic Football Pitch outside of Ireland. We'd play up there on the weekends and of course, at that time, they were drinking. That's a bad mix. The usual county pride, with strong drink, would break into animosity for those not of their county. It was brutal. There is an old joke, that someone went to a fight and a hockey game broke out. Well, sometimes, a football match broke out. No matter where you play, Cork, Wembley Stadium, or on a farm, the motto is the same, "hell for leather for one hour."

Playing in the U.S. was good, but unfortunately, the standard was not that of the motherland and a bigger hindrance was that there were not as many games or as many teams. I also missed the "Irish Brogue" all over the field. I can still see my brother, Sean, streaking down the pitch. He played for Ulster. And, the Mighty McGraths live on with my nephew Marty, now an All Star. Deep down in my heart and soul, Gaelic Football lives inside of me. Playing with other Irish immigrants in great cities like Philadelphia, Boston, Chicago, San Francisco, and many others, I was always so proud to see the Irish Flag flying against the beautiful American sky.

7

The Troubles

On September 23, 1971, I graduated with a Certificate of Education issued by Queens University, Belfast. Where was I going to go with my life? I got a job as a teacher in training. On my first day, I asked the kids to go home and draw anything they had a mind to. "Use your imagination," I said. I wanted those kids to come alive. They all looked shell shocked by the violence around them at that time. The next day, a kid showed up with a flag he had drawn. All hell broke loose over that and soon I was in the front office. Those days were very difficult times.

"The Troubles" in the North of Ireland began in the late 1960s and was internationally known as "The Northern Ireland Conflict." Its aim was to end discrimination against the minority, who were Catholic Nationalists. They had been trampled on for too long by the Protestant Unionists and the police force. The Troubles lasted for 30 years with all sorts of violence escalating throughout the North. Some acts of violence spread to the Republic of Ireland (The South), to England, and to the continent of Europe, sometimes classified as a "guerrilla or low level war."

The whole island of Ireland has 32 different counties, six in the North under British Rule and 26 in the South under the Republic of Ireland. The Unionists or Loyalists, who were mostly Protestant, wanted to stay under British rule. On the other hand, Irish Nationalists and Republicans, who were mostly Catholics, wanted to join with the Republic of Ireland. In other words, they wanted to be done with colonization and unite with the rest of Ireland. War, no matter on what level, is not a pretty thing and not everyone, be they Catholic or Protestant, was in favor of The Troubles.

Life in rural areas, for the most part, carried on as usual with sporadic violence, here and there. In the populated areas, such as Belfast and Derry City, among others, it was a completely different ball game. As in any war, things got extremely nasty and downright ugly. Having been born on a country farm and educated in a big city, namely Belfast, I saw all sides of this war from '69 to '71. I knew the ins and outs of a tank as well as I did a Volkswagen.

War stories are not bedtime stories. Sights linger for a lifetime. They influence the formation of your character. When war begins, normal life is completely lost. Lives change. They have to, and drastically.

In the North, the conflict was mostly political, despite the religious differences between the groups. We had a lot of paramilitary groups, both Catholic and Protestant all around us. These groups were very serious people with their own set missions. Also, right in the middle of the conflict, we had the politicians and activists, voicing their opinions, some peaceful, others not so much. The Republic of Ireland's security forces, in the end, played a very small role.

"The Good Friday Agreement" in 1998 seemed to end The Troubles, but at a very high cost of human life. Around 3,500 or more had paid the ultimate price. The victims were mainly civilians. The agreement did not bring complete peace. Sporadic violence still erupted throughout the North. As a student teacher in '69, in Belfast, I saw it all. The first thing you noticed was the death of anything that was fun. How could you have fun, when all hell had broken loose? Army checkpoints sprang up, everywhere. Guns were always in sight, ready to serve their terrible purpose. If you were in a vehicle, you were searched. If you went

33

shopping, you were frisked. This caused conflict. Commands at gunpoint cause tense questions to be ignored and spat upon. It was a pot boiling over. It was just a matter of time. Happy days became sad as gray skies clouded the sunbeams. Friends drifted apart, factioning along political or religious lines. Catholics grouped with Catholics and Protestants did likewise. Barbed wire fences replaced flower beds and gardens, and silence fell like a blanket over the natural joy of the Northern Irish.

Darkness is a phenomenon. Bad things can happen there and so it did with The Troubles. Violent acts disappeared into the darkness, leaving only the echo of life lost. Neighbor distrusted neighbor. Paranoia set in. Social life was a calculated risk. Bars were now bomb targets. Cars were loaded with explosives and when they exploded, they left a wake of carnage like in any other war. Body parts were scattered over the streets as students and workers tried to maintain some semblance of normality.

Wearing different color clothes could cost you your life. Walking into the wrong area at the wrong time, could take you out of this world. Your religion could cost you the ultimate, your life. Your name could cost you the ultimate, your life. "Where do you go to school, lad?" Never answer that, it could cost you. "What area are you from," a question that used to bring us together, now singled the Irish out as if in front of a firing line. No matter who was right or who was wrong, no matter how one worshiped God, this was a sad state of humanity. Fear can be nearly impossible to communicate, but you can see it in the eyes and it was everywhere, as was anger and terrible sadness. One day after school, I saw kids playing with spent bullets like toys.

The social repercussions were massive, especially with the children and young adults. The bombings, the fires, the checkpoints, and the constant military presence branded young minds. The side effect of all this was an old demon the Irish have known too well and for far too long, poverty. As the old saying goes, "when poverty comes through the

Derry City during The Troubles

Soldiers on the streets of Derry City

door, love flies out the window." Suicides, murders, vandalism, all increased as did the homeless. While I was in Belfast in 1970, there were over 10,000 vandalized homes, sitting empty, alone. The vandals were mostly between the ages of eight and 13. Think about that. From 1969 to 1998, 3,635 people were killed and 257 of these were under the age of 17.

You can't be ready for it. I surely wasn't. But, it was right there in front of me in the paper:

> There is a mixture of horror and anger among the Fermanagh majority at Thursday night's killing with a shot fired by the police of an unarmed inoffensive young Donegal cattle dealer, 22-year-old Michael Joseph Leonard, a few yards on the Northern side of the border of Fermanagh and Donegal.

It only took one shot and my cousin and best friend was dead. We grew up together, ran through the fields together, and played football together. He taught me a special love of farm animals.

Serious questions about his death were raised. He was driving to his home in the South of Ireland, followed by a police Land Rover just yards into the North of Ireland. On May 17, 1973, one shot rang out and his car stopped. A short time later, Michael died in the hospital, in his father Maurice's arms.

According to reports, he had a disqualified driver's license in the North of Ireland, but valid in the South of Ireland. Why on this Earth would you kill another human being for a disqualified driver's license? It was a matter of a few yards. Why? Why would you take the life of a young hardworking farmer? All he wanted to do was to buy and sell cattle, that's all. To this day, I still wonder, as do many, and every yard I run has a life of its own.

8

Coming To The U.S.

I had to go somewhere, had to do something, something new. My feet were itchier than ever. Actually, my mother was born in America, in Philadelphia to be exact, but came to Ireland as a very little girl. I told her I wanted to go back to America, which meant to live, perhaps for good, and she smiled at me in such a deep way that only a mother can, and said, "you are going to see the land where I was born." It sure seemed like all arrows pointed to America and all it represented.

My first trip to America had been on June 16, 1969, soaring 35,000 feet above the United States of America, the massive 747 was better than being on Air Force One. It brought over 300 passengers to the land of the free, home of the brave. What a flight! First time on a plane for me. There was excitement in every seat, joy on every face, not a worry in the world, all going to join the "hippie world."

When we touched down at Kennedy Airport, a cheer went up. The first thing I felt was a massive heat wave. We just don't have those in Ireland. It was downright tropical. For the first time I saw people of all races in one spot. It was my first time to see so many big people, first time to use a passport, and the first time to be surrounded by skinheads all chanting "Hare Krishna." What we saw on TV was really happening on the streets of America. I was totally bamboozled. Even the size of the cars was shocking to me from mini to 20 foot convertibles and everybody was in a mad rush. Where they were all going, I had no idea, but it seemed to my ears, they were all screaming. It was a far cry from sheep and goats sneezing and grunting on the farm. Life had flipped like a bar table in just a seven-hour flight. The car bombs, explosions, and shootings in Belfast were shaken off like dust in the wind of that airplane.

I listened to my mother and brought a heavy coat. I always listened to my mother. I didn't always do what she said, but I listened. This time, maybe I shouldn't have. It was scorching hot, but New York was stunning. "Sweet Caroline" played every 5 minutes. The choices of radio and TV stations were staggering. At home there were only two. I fell in love with convertible cars and had to have one. It took some time, but I later achieved that dream.

Drive-in movies were unheard of in Ireland. What a grand thing! The subways were baffling and there were more yellow cabs than raindrops. Long hair was freely accepted and drugs were rampant. It was 1969, a famous or infamous year in American History, depending on your beliefs. There was the moon landing and there were the Manson murders. My first meal was a cheeseburger and fries and it is still my favorite. I was now getting french fries on a plate, not chips wrapped in a newspaper.

I'd never imagined New York was as large as it was. It wasn't like going to another country, it was like stepping off on the moon. This was the '60s, but instead of discovering free love and rambling about butt naked, I found the love of running.

I was there with a Gaelic Football Team. At that time, I still hadn't taken up drinking yet, so while the other lads were off at the pub, I waited in a park in Queens. After an hour of them not showing up, I got so bored I thought I would go for a run. Three hours later, they showed up, drunk. I ran the whole time and I loved it. It was simple and I could do it on my own, anytime I wanted.

Coming back to New York for the second time in 1971, there was a different feeling. I was moving there. I needed to find a way to live.

People come to New York and they look up at those great buildings and they say "I can't do it." When you come to New York, everything is difficult, getting a place to live, finding a job, even opening a checking account. Me being a Gaelic Footballer made things a lot easier. A meeting was arranged in a parking lot among the Irish and the Irish Americans. I showed up and became a "wire lather," a steel fixer, by the shake of a hand. A piece of paper got me into the union, temporarily, for the summer months. The Irish blood took care of their own.

Jobs could last days or weeks, depending on the size. Construction was not my love in life, mainly because it was not steady. Between jobs I had a unique experience trying to be a "sand hog." This is real work. I went with my friend, Frank Quinn, and showed up for work. Sand hogs dig into the Earth, burrowing out paths for subways and tunnels. They go underneath rivers, buildings, and whatever stands in their way. It is an extremely dangerous job, even for experienced workers and that I wasn't. You have to be compressed and decompressed, when you go down and up from the pit of the Earth. If you don't, you will get the "bends," which can be fatal. You cannot mess with the blood flow. "A man was killed yesterday, so we need one of you to go down," said the foreman to Frank and me. I started to shake, even as tough as I thought I was. The care taker in the changing hut was from home in Ireland and said to me, "don't go down there, you might not come back up." There was a cold seriousness in his eyes and voice. I let Frank do the dirty work. When he got down, he was shocked to see a lot of alcohol involved. Bottles of whiskey in the back pockets and dynamite in the walls is not a good combination. For Frank, one shift was enough. For me, getting a job on solid ground seemed a little difficult for a while. I was sent to the sewer in Brooklyn to install the steel rods, before pouring the concrete. I was literally in the bowels of the Earth and it seemed everybody was "dumping on me." Again, alcohol was consumed to drown the stench, but I did not complain. I was still an immigrant. In fact, I was let go. "I gotta throw you outta the sewer, Tom," the man in charge told me.

The fact was that someone had to go. There were too many hands. There was a difference between an Irish American and an immigrant. They came first and I was at the bottom of the list. "I couldn't very well keep you and throw one of them out, now could I. I'm sorry," and like that I was kicked out of the city's toilet.

In construction, they had great respect for the Irish, but I had to lie a bit to get a good one.

"You ever done steel fixing before?" a man, who I took it to be my boss asked me.

"Ya," I said.

"Where?"

"Philadelphia," I said.

Well, next thing I know, they put a belt on me and a pair of nippers. I'd never had a belt in my life, except the kind you get from misbehaving. It was 98 degrees. I was in shorts, sweating like a pig and I hadn't done anything, yet. "It's a rat race upstairs," says he. This is how naive I was. I was looking up for the rats. They sent me to bring up some deck chairs. Those kept the steel rods off the concrete. I came back and said I couldn't find any deck chairs. I was looking for something you could sit in and have a glass of lemonade. So, then I'm up 14 flights in the air. There is an art to this steel fixing business, now. It's a one, two, three action. You tie and clip off the steel rebar in the concrete, while walking along this wooden beam. All the while you have yourself clipped to the beam. We started off and within 18 seconds the guy I started with was 3 feet ahead of me. By the time lunch came, I'd gone about 5 feet.

One day, I saw a man moving down the lumber. He was unhooking from the crane when he went out over the edge. It was slow motion. I can see it, now. He was spread out in the air like an eagle. There was no elevator, so I ran down 14 flights of stairs. When I got down, there was a nun already over him, kneeling beside him. I stood there, stunned. I prayed and went and sat with the other workers. Thirty minutes later, we were all back to work.

Drinking was a different thing in America, I noticed. One thing that shocked me to my core was the Irish were going into bars for a "brute of a sandwich and a beer." That never happened in Ireland. People went to bars at night, if they happened to have a bit of money. I couldn't understand it, having a beer with food. It's totally against my taste buds. I later learned that it was crucial to bar business in the United States, but more importantly, I learned that the Irish living in the U.S. were different than they were back home.

The infamous white house

In 1972, I bought a Bonneville for $400. It was my first car and the biggest machine I've ever owned in my life. The owner was returning to Ireland for good and he literally gave me his registration, license plates, and his driver's license. Back then, Irish Driver's Licenses didn't have photos. To me, it could have been a gold medal. What a feeling that was to turn that key in my own car! I had total freedom to drive around, anywhere that I wanted, but of course it was illegal.

America, in my eyes, must have been a lot like those settlers that first crossed over those Sierra Mountains and beheld California. There was plenty of food. There were beautiful women everywhere the eye could see. Lively music played on every corner and there was an immense atmosphere that surrounded you, that said "welcome."

We lived in the "white house." That's what we called it, 'cause it was white as marble. Paddy Diamond got it for us. We were all Irish and we rented the whole building, so to us, it was indeed a presidential hotel. There were male and female guests all over the place. I talked to everyone, "Hi, my name is Herbie. What's yours?" That was a nickname I'd picked up in Ireland and it stuck. After coming home from work in the evenings, we'd go for a seven or eight mile run and then a workout in our basement, which we had converted into a makeshift gym. The weights and materials were all garnered from the construction sites we worked at. It was simple as could be, but raw and beautiful.

We had a black and white TV, which had such great shows as "The F Troup," "Gilligan's Island," "Hogan's Heroes," and "Sanford and Son." We'd finish off the night with "The Honeymooners" and "Burns and Allen." The nature of those TV Shows, and this may sound childish, was a major tool of cultural adjustment for us. Every day, we laughed our hearts out and it countered the negativity that would come across on the news channels, along with images of horrible violence back home in Ireland.

They say birds of a feather flock together and that was so true in our case. New Year's Day, 1973, Seamus Donaghy and myself set out to make our first million. We bid everybody a goodbye and drove to the George Washington Bridge. There, we tossed a coin. Heads was west to California. Tails was south to Florida. Florida it was, and my Bonneville was our traveling hotel. Seamus was bigger than I, so he had the honor of sleeping in the backseat, while I nestled in the front. We headed off on this "freedom ride" with a whopping $600, everything illegal, and not a worry in the world. Johnny Cash, Merle Haggard, and John Denver were our companions and fortunately for us, not a cop in sight. It was liberty at its best. We were heading nowhere in particular, just where the steering wheel turned.

I'll never forget the town of Jesup, Georgia. We were greeted by a massive 6-foot-6 police Sheriff. His accent was as strong as his words, "In the State of Georgia, you don't tell me, I tell you. Get that headlight fixed at that gas station over there or I will lock you up. You understand?" That put the fear of God in me and I responded in a mousy voice "yes sir." We booked into the first motel we saw there. I didn't trust that officer and it worried me with my legal status. We headed over to the nearest bar, which turned out to be a gin mill. It was clear out of towners didn't sit well there, so we had no choice but to make a retreat. We had no idea who was married, who was single, or who was carrying a gun. They eyed us like a couple of rabid foxes.

Fourteen-hundred miles from the start, we landed in Miami. There had been no handcuffs and no fights. It was an utter success. A million smiles and even more swimming pools greeted us with open arms. We'd soon find out the thrills and dangers that freedom and opportunity provide.

9

Unknown Places

Soon after arriving in Miami, we developed a system. Using the car as a motel could only last so long, so we started showing up at random swimming pools. We'd walk up and say hello. Our Irish accents were a big plus and we'd take advantage. A pool party was made that much more fun with a couple of scalding white Irishmen with big accents. To us, it was a shower. We'd jump in the pool, clean off good, and head off again. They were none the wiser.

I finally got a job selling hamburgers. The only problem was, I was not a chef and we had no customers. Only my buddy Seamus would show up, and I couldn't take his money. We'd both have a couple of burgers and when the boss showed up after an hour, I knew the gig was up. "You don't have to pay me," I said, "cause the burgers are in my belly." We were back to being beach bums and the million smiles started to fade.

Luck showed up at our feet once again. While heading back to the beach, one early afternoon, a beautiful young lady approached me. Sitting on the sand, the conversation came around to employment. This was music to my ears. "Would you like to sell Bibles and Magazines?" she asked. She informed me the job was off in Puerto Rico and the ticket, hotel, and meals would be free, along with some pay.

She had a beautiful smile and a chipper positive attitude. I was really getting the hang of this land of opportunity. You just had to put yourself out there. "When can we start?" was my reply. I was licking my chops. This was better than we'd ever hoped for. "You can fly out tonight," she said. I couldn't believe it. The million smiles were back on our horizon and wider than ever.

After touching down in Puerto Rico, we were met by a couple of, what I took to be, shady characters. They took us to a swanky joint and treated us to a steak dinner with all the trimmings. As good as the steak was, I couldn't get over the fact that we were eating in some kind of bordello. I never saw so many women walking around in next to nothing in my entire life. Bibles and brothels didn't mix in Ireland and I wasn't sure if they should anywhere. I closed my eyes to that as best I could, well partially, as I was in desperate need of protein and that steak was almighty good.

Next, we arrived at the Borinquen Hotel in San Juan. It looked like an oasis from the hardships of the world, aqua blue and white, right on the shore. The only problem was, it wasn't a resort at all, at least for us. In actuality, it would become a prison.

They had rules and regulations out the wazoo. In bed at 10, up at 5:30, on the road at 8:30 and sell what was supposed to be Bibles. On Wednesday and Saturday nights, we could stay out till midnight, and then there was no drinking, no drugs, and no gambling. We had unknowingly joined up with a cult. The second day, after not having sold a single Bible, I took the mind to enjoy it while it lasted. I'd knock on a door and say "My name is Tom. Would you like to buy a Bible?" "Me don't speak English," was always the response. "Me don't speak Spanish," I'd say as the door slammed. I'd go back and play pool, which I knew would be trouble.

Sell no Bibles, bring in no money, and you are gonna get the axe. This was a real possibility in our minds as we were called to the boss' office, who was basically a gangster. For one, the man was using some sort of false name. We knew it was not going to be good and could be violent, but we needed the money for our time. Funds were running low and being in a foreign land, we were ready to punch our way out if necessary. We were Irish, grew up rough, and we'd drop the hammer on any bugger that tried to squelch on a deal. But, he had a pistol. So, with hands in our pockets and tails between our legs, we two athletic boxers, slumped our way out the door. We were now homeless and as they used to say "broke as a joke."

Queens, New York, 1972

We couldn't get a lick of work. The language barrier, alone, was insurmountable. There wasn't a Consulate for the Irish, so we went to the British Consulate with a hard luck story of losing our money in the hotel and begged for the money to get us back to the mainland. It worked. We surrendered our passports and cut a deal back to New York, where we'd have to pay them back. Time to start, again. There is an old saying in Ireland "If you have enough feathers in your hat, you will be able to fly home, free." Well, I had another feather. That's all I can say about that.

Paddy Reilly was his name. He was a friend, who owned a bar in Queens. "Tom," he says, "how would you like to own a bar?" I hit the bar with my hand and said I'd give all I had to own my own bar. He said, "how would you like to own my brother's bar?" I replied, "that sounds great, the only problem is, I don't have any money."

I never thought my life would go that way. I never thought I'd leave Ireland, never thought I would work in sewers and skyscrapers, and absolutely never thought I would take a drink. My path didn't start anywhere near that direction. I was set down a path laid by my mother and siblings and that was to take the Orders. I was an athlete as a toddler and taught physical education as a young adult. Exercise was life.

"Okay, give me the bar."

10

Bar Business

For the first time in my life, I had a chance to own my own business, be my own boss, and perhaps make something of myself. Paddy cut me a deal and gave me the bar for $32,000. I had $600 and I gave it to him. He took it and told me I was now a bar owner. That's a business deal between the Irish. It's a simple thing. You don't have the money now, but I know you to be a good man and I've got no worries. No need to even shake hands. Those deals could happen back then, never today.

I didn't really know the bar. It was called "Reilly and Tully's" and it was out in Jamaica Queens, which in the '70s, wasn't one of your safest neighborhoods. That didn't bother me so much, coming from the North, but nothing in my life had prepared me for what I saw the next day.

When you walk in a place in the daytime, you see things you don't see at night. When the lights are low, the booze is swimming in your blood, and people are all about the place. It's metaphorical, actually, of what alcoholics do with their lives. They turn their own lights down and look away from the dirty bits.

As I walked in, I didn't recall all the holes in the floor. There was a woman sitting at the far end of the bar. She had a bowl of raw meat, a cat beside her, and she was having an early morning whiskey. She was feeding the cat the raw meat and taking some bites, herself. Her name was Rosie and she was a daytime regular, I was told. So was former boxing champ, Willy Banjo. As I walked to the back, he was in the watering hole and punched the door open. He could have knocked me out with that. The bar sat just one mile from Creedmoor Mental Hospital and many of their outpatients were our inpatients. They lived in homes nearby, set up by the health care system.

It was now my bar and it was a chance at doing something on my own terms. I stacked six cases of beer up in a corner and laid a piece of plywood over it. We had a stage. I got a jukebox, a shuffle board, then a pool table for $100. Most importantly, I filled the bar with Irish girls, so it appealed to Irish people and all the locals. In those days, Irish bartenders would support you. They would come to your bar and buy rounds for everyone. In turn, you'd do the same. Within a few weeks, the bar was packed and we had a blast. I realized, early on, that everyone wants to meet the owner. I made sure I knew everyone that came in and they knew me. People are the key.

There were several rooms, upstairs. I rented them out, two men per room. They were mostly in their '60s and had seen better days. They would pay with their Social Security checks. I would cash them for them. In many ways they couldn't afford it, but I took care of them. I would buy them underwear and socks and cut their hair. I invented the punk hairdo long before it came into fashion. We were the happiest family in Queens. Those were the best of times. I got my green card and met my wife, but as the book says, it was also the worst of times. It was then, that I started to drink.

When I bought Reilly and Tully's Bar, it was an investment in America, but a tough and rough proposition with the bullets and dollars flying in all directions. Thanks be to God, no one was ever hurt, even though guns were plentiful. In the early '70s, there were no metal detectors, no pat downs, no security guard out front, just the old fashion way, the discretion of the bartender. I always like to try to put the good

49

before the bad, so about the dollars flying, I meant that I became legal, after going through the process of buying the bar. Those licenses, alone, can sink you. Today, a liquor license in New York can cost you 50 big ones or more, right up front. Back then, one had to invest $10,000 and apply for legal status, which I did with the help and generosity of a bar owner called Alan Clancy. Guns and alcohol really do not mix and when you get a liquor license and you put that shiny plaque on the wall, you don't have a certificate in gun control. People will carry a gun, legal or not. I heard some customers call my bar "the bucket of blood." That was upsetting.

On one particular occasion, I called the bar and the bartender, Peter McGuinness, answered the phone. "Everything okay?" I asked. "Business is good," said he, "everything is quite peaceful now. Quite a few people here watching the cops up on ladders trying to get the bullets out of the ceiling." Peter's voice was as calm as a dad reading bedtime stories to his little one, "just a wee bit of shooting. Bad shots, those. Bullets went into the ceiling. Anyway, no one got killed, which is good. Other than that, everything is under control." He couldn't have sounded calmer. Just another day at Reilly and Tully's. The fighters and shooters were gone, again, never to be found.

Owning a bar in New York City is a very special privilege and as a former bar owner told me, "once you receive your first liquor license, you have entered the wildest side of life on this planet." "Why?" I asked. "Because, there is wine, women, and song." Those words turned out to be so true and they all go together, hand in hand. We all know that to some degree selling whiskey is like selling a legalized drug which if not taken in moderation can become highly addictive. I am the living proof of that, the perfect example, unfortunately.

To obtain a liquor license in New York, one must go through rigid investigations and many background checks. To name a few, financial and conduct checks are required. Any misconduct, for example being convicted of a felony, will warrant a refusal of a license.

Owning a bar comes with a lot of important responsibilities. To a certain degree, you have the power of the customers lives in your hands. For the "regular" customer, the owner is a major player in their well being and their health, serving them is at the discretion of the bar. Moderation has high priority at all times. A path of destruction can happen before your eyes to those who consume alcohol on a daily basis.

Manning my first bar, Reilly and Tully's

Upon receiving a liquor license, you automatically have an honors degree in politics and a degree in almost all walks of life. Sooner or later, you will hear everything because when, "the wine is in, the wit is out." It's all a part of the job, being a bar owner in the greatest city in the world. Every day is a special day and every night is unique. Anything and everything can happen. People are predictable, yet so unpredictable. The most personal secrets can come flying out at any second. Tears can mop the bar. Laughter can lift the roof. Loneliness can be so obvious and alcohol can be so beautifully ugly. Every sip creates a different reaction in different people. But, honestly, I have to say that a real authentic Irish bar in the middle of New York City is a gem, a priceless piece of property that can bring so much joy to the world. Spreading joy is very noble, but truthfully, it sometimes can come at a very high cost.

Years ago, among the Irish bar owners in New York, there was an unwritten tradition. You visit my bar, spend a few dollars and I will visit your bar and spend a few of my dollars. I did that, regularly. Quite often leading to a large consumption of alcohol, spending hour after hour, basically talking non-sense, but at the time, we all thought it was great fun. We all knew that when we walked into a true, authentic, Irish bar in New York, we were walking on the "Blarney Stone" and the recipient of pure blarney, good and bad, sad and happy. One thing for certain, the Irish can give a "great line." Most have the gift of the gab. Unfortunately, I know for a fact that numerous Irish bar owners, personal friends, paid the ultimate price. They drank themselves to death. I was there. I was at their wakes. I was at the funerals. I knelt at the caskets and the main conversation was, "it is terrible he drank himself to death. He was a great man." What a price to pay and to be real honest, I put a big down payment on my own deathbed, only with God's help to replace the funeral home with the gym and running during the early '90s.

I've always had itchy feet. I would stay with a bar for a few years and move on. It's just my nature. I originally leased out my first bar to train for my '77 cross country run. Later, just because I needed a new start. In '91, I landed a bar on the upper east side, just across from Fox 5 News. It was there, that I started to go downhill, seriously. I gained weight when I was on a drinking binge. I would get up to 260 pounds from 140. I wouldn't eat while I was drinking. It interfered with my drinking. I would wait till I came home and eat everything in the fridge. I'd leave pistachio nuts scattered everywhere. I was a tornado when I came home and left a lot of destruction.

I loved all the bars that I owned in the city. It's a special love of an inanimate object that only bar owners can feel or realize the depth of. The daily love that flows the second you turn the key, no matter what conditions the bar is left in from the night before. It is a new day and only time will tell what that day brings. No matter what, there will be happiness, fun and joy. That's the beauty of alcohol, when it's not abused. The atmosphere will develop, music will increase, voices get louder and a family of unusual diversity will be created, each day, before your eyes. What a beautiful feeling and as an owner, it's all mine. The bar is the creation and reflection of the owner. It is his personality taken over by all nationalities of the world. It can be smooth, great, and exhilarating. Also, it can be dangerous, ruthless and lethal.

Looking back, I have come to realize one of my beautiful bars brought me to my knees, literally. Physically and mentally, it brought me down, gently and with utmost discretion. It was like a smiling bulldozer with the throttle running wide open on alcohol. It scattered my brains with booze. It was a bulldozer ride, an expensive one, and it rode me right into New York University Hospital. The bar was located on the upper east side and frequented by all nationalities, creeds, and walks of life. It was one of the most intellectual bars I've ever owned. Business men, media personalities, doctors, lawyers, and athletes of every sport were daily regulars. It was also, surprisingly, one of the wildest Manhattan has had the pleasure to rest on its soil. It was here, that I dedicated a portion of my life to the absolute abuse of alcohol. The bar was named *Tom McGrath's*.

11

My Olympics

From age 7, my Olympics were the local, annual, Parish sport's day. It was the only day of the year that my heart raced, adrenaline flew, and excitement boiled over and I competed in every event possible. Sitting around the hearth fire in the late '50s, my father would vividly tell us how many races he won. He was proud. We could see it in those eyes of his that would light up when he talked about it. He crossed the finish line first in the 100 yard, 220 yard, and 440 yard races. As soon as I got out of my "nappie," I wanted to win, just like my dad. He said, "I was like a flash of lightning."

The sports day was organized by the Catholic Church and The G.A.A., and took place on any level field, in those days. Weather permitting, this ancient tradition was a beautiful sight to behold. Young athletes came to local fame and were the conversation piece until the next one.

There were all sorts of events. No clocks. No measuring tapes. Just the cow grass and the competitors, mad to go. We had long and short races: the sack race, three-legged races, egg and spoon races, even pillow fighting. There was a dog race, which was purely a dog fight. Farm dogs don't give a damn about a fake rabbit. They went straight for each other. Then there was the Donkey Derby. Most farm donkeys have never had a homosapien on their backs. Mine landed me on my ass in 5 seconds, granting me the record for the shortest recorded run. The only jockey experience I had was on pigs. I used to hop on a pig, my feet touching the ground for balance and off I'd go. This always ended in a scolding. My father would yell at me to no end, "you'll break his living back."

The first ultramarathon in Ireland, late 1970s

The tug of war amazed me, big heavy locals pulling a rope. Their weather beaten faces got so red and at the end, they all plummeted to the ground in exhaustion. It was something to see those huge anchor men use all that strength. While this was going on, there was a cycle race on the outside and a G.A.A. match on the infield.

I entered every event possible. I won some and lost some, but always had winning on my mind. None of our family or the locals could beat my oldest brother, Anthony. Like my father, he was a streak of lightning across those fields. It was in those days, that the Mighty McGraths were truly born. That was the one day out of the year, when there was no religion. People from all walks of life came together from miles around to meet, greet, and compete. Sport has a way of doing that. Traditional Irish music by the Ederney Pipe Band piped away and everyone enjoyed sandwiches. When your father winks at you with your medals and says, "good boys, you're keeping the family tradition goin," it's hard to find a greater joy. It was tattooed on my soul and even in the busiest bar in New York City, I longed for sport.

12

The '77 Run

The idea first entered my mind in '76. I went to Montreal to the Olympic Games. If that doesn't inspire you, not much will. Lasse Viren became the only runner to date to repeat as Olympic champion in the 5,000 meters. It was a spectacular race. He was challenged several times in the last lap. Each time a runner came shoulder to shoulder with him, he lowered his chin and sprinted forward. There were four runners just behind him, fighting to catch him at the finish line. One man dove, trying to get third place, but it was Viren that out sprinted the world. He also repeated as champion in the 10,000 meters, but placed fifth in the Marathon, failing to repeat Emile Zatopek's trifecta.

Leon Spinks and Sugar Ray Leonard both won gold medals in boxing. Shun Fujimoto finished his routine on the rings with a triple somersault dismount, scoring a 9.7 and a victory for Japan. Only later, we found out he did it with a broken knee. I saw a man shatter the world record in the decathlon, one of the toughest events in all of sport. He was then known as Bruce Jenner. Such feats. Such pride in country and sport. I had to do something. I needed a challenge. I decided I would not only run across the United States, I would break the world record.

"Limbo" is a real place. It is what happens to the body when you run

15 to 18 hours a day, and 3,046 miles is a long time for the body to stay in limbo. New York to San Francisco. It was a crazy idea. Would years of physical and mental training be enough? It would be a mighty feat on feet. Massive body changes are inevitable; being your own doctor and psychiatrist is a must. Time is of the essence and this run would be a rare full-time, nonpaying job.

A 3,000 mile run would be the run of a lifetime for anyone, but for me, it was also my honeymoon. The day before, Mena and I made a bond together that would last a lifetime. My brother, Father Sean McGrath, did the honors in front of 300 happy guests. It was August 28, 1977, Queens, New York, and the world was a great smile. The next day we were on the road. With a start at City Hall, City Council President, Paul O'Dwyer, made me an honorary mail man. As a fellow Irishman and friend, he gave me a task, "off you go me lad and deliver this letter to City Hall, San Francisco. We are on a budget. We'll save the price of a stamp. Good luck." It was 90 degrees and tears mixed with sweat as family and friends disappeared behind me. It was on. My honeymoon on the run had begun.

In your mind, you have to put the idea of breaking the record to the side, when you get down to business. My only concern was that every time I put my foot down, it came back up the same way, injury free. Gary Murke had shown up at my door before the run. Gary was the first winner of the New York City Marathon. At that time, it was run in Central Park. Gary later bought a van and would park it around 96th street and Fifth Avenue. He sold shoes there to all the runners. Back then, there weren't many good spots to get good shoes. So, the night before my run, he showed up with 10 pairs of New Balance. To make any successful journey happen, you need kindness. Without it, no matter how talented you are, you will come up short and bitter.

Crossing the George Washington Bridge, carrying the Irish Flag with 3,000 miles ahead of me, I couldn't have been more full of life. Behind me, my wife and two friends, Jimmy Mannion, a mechanic, and Richie Barberi, a medic, trailed in a Winnebago. It was another act of kindness that proved indispensable, donated by Alan Clancy. Another donation was a little red moped. While the Winnebago would go ahead several miles, the moped could stay near with water and supplies. In New Jersey, it got blistering hot and I had to strip off my shirt. If it stayed as hot as this, I wondered if I'd ever make it. Before I'd gotten 20 miles out, a man pulls along side me in a truck, actually forcing me over into the grass. "You look strong and fit. Could you do me a favor?" he asked. I couldn't imagine, what on Earth I could do for anybody at that particular point in time. "Could you help me move some furniture?" his eyes squinted as he looked close for my reply. With sweat pouring off me, I told him I couldn't, that I was on my way to California. He looked like a spurned lover, "what," he said, and took off like a bat out of hell.

My wife was the main stabilizer, taking care of the mobile home, food, laundry, which is a big issue on long runs, the shoes and gear, etc. Jim did the driving and Ricky was the moped man. On occasion, Mena would show up on the moped and that was priceless. I needed that more than she knew, because I rarely show the turmoil that's burning inside me. When asked by an interviewer if I ever thought about quitting, I responded, "every five minutes." That was not a joke. It was an understatement. Constantly, I fought off the urge, the simple urge, to just stop. Because of that, I liked to run in silence. The loneliness was a place, where I could secretly battle with myself to push on. I could focus, feel the rhythm, and conserve energy. That was key as there was massive media coverage, that added onto the stress of the run, itself. On top of that, it was my honeymoon and that has its own set of pressures. No rest for the wicked, they say.

The northeast, especially New Jersey and Pennsylvania, set me off to a rough start. There was the heat, the deafening traffic, the knock you down wind from the trucks, lumps of tires on the roadside, and bottles and cans littered between every step. It's hard to like a monster, but I had to. On the first day, I was grazed by a truck. They were basically going to escort me the whole 3,000 miles, so I made peace with them in my mind; big protectors that were running along with me, watching my back. They dubbed me "the little red rabbit" on their CB's because of the red moped, and that went a long way for me to change a negative into a positive. Every ounce of positive you can find, you hold onto on the back roads of America. We could hear them chatting on our CB in the mobile home, "we cannot see the red rabbit's ears," "he doesn't wag his tail," and "we don't want rabbit soup." They would blow their horns as they came by me and that is encouragement you can feel in your bones.

I knew that two main concerns were going to be dogs and humans. The first being rather predictable and the second, not so much. I was surprised to find a greater adversary out there, that I was totally unprepared for. It was after crossing over the mountains of Pennsylvania and running through West Virginia in just over an hour, that I met my real foe, the grasshopper. They defended their cornfield territory with a vengeance. I must have knocked a thousand off my legs. This takes you out of your stride and can start to cause strain in your back. The suckers must have thought my sweat was the nectar of the gods, as they would latch on and try to hitch a ride as long as possible. They were such a pest, that I had to move to the middle of the road. The little buggers.

Dogs were not as bad as I had imagined. I carried mace with me and only had to pull it four or five times. You have to be quick on the draw, for they can come on you like a tiger out of the bush. The last thing I wanted was to explain in an interview how a dog had put me out of the running.

People proved to be a worthy adversary, as expected. Day one, the furniture mover, had shown that. While running across, what seemed like endless cornfields, nature called. This is something ultra runners know all too well. You've got to find spots to be free with your toilet. In the cornfields, that was easy enough to do. You just dipped into the cover a good 10 or 15 yards and did your business. One day, a young lad, I can say this as I clearly saw his bushy little hairdo in the cockpit, started buzzing me in his crop duster. Trying to answer the call of nature, while zigzagging away from an overzealous pilot was an adventure. He was as determined as I was. In the end, I believe I contributed to the following year's crop.

I forced myself to drink every two to three miles. You have to. Many times you don't want to. You may gain a few seconds pushing on, but lose a few hours or even days in the end. Dehydration is a sleeping tiger, that creeps up on you very slowly. He's on you with all his fangs before you know it. All endurance runners know you don't experiment with anything new. Advice can come from all angles, but deflect it you must. A fantastic energy boost for one is a toilet stopper for another. No steak. No spicy food. I drank while standing as not to choke and ate while walking. Baby food worked well and similar substances, that go down easily and are quickly digested.

Every minute detail was crucial. Socks, for example, were a major focus. One crease can cause a blister. If infection comes, you're out. I've seen many wet eyes of great runners carried from the track. My wife kept the socks powdered and cared for. The toe nails have to be kept extremely trim. They will act up in a heartbeat and cause you some of the most irritating pain you'll find. God was good to me and gave me good, tough feet. That may be my strongest suit.

Jimmy, we found out, had a sleeping disorder. In a cramped mobile home, this became a deal breaker. A little sawing noise is one thing, but standing outside, frustrated from sleeplessness and fatigue, watching the mobile home slowly rock side to side like a house boat on the water, is another. We were a family on that trip, all four of us, but my wife and I had to check into motels on several occasions to get some sleep. The Epsom salt baths were a godsend and in the rooms, I could use my electric heating pads with no worry. Unfortunately, once we got into the deserts, there were no motels. There wasn't anything for what seemed like days on end. We decided, for some reason, to camp out. It seemed like the thing to do. The crew built a little campfire and they played some country music. I slept while they partied.

As soon as the fire was out and Jimmy was back in the home, it was rocking again, and I found myself outside at 4 a.m., agitated. I rolled up in a blanket and tried to sleep on the sand, no go. I couldn't get the idea of a snake coming up on me out of my head. I was terrified of them. St. Patrick had never gone a chasing in the wild west, and perhaps the snakes wanted revenge on a sleepy little Irishman. With one eye open, I saw the sun start to bring in the day and I took off running. I took some food and water, but let everyone else sleep. There was only one road. They would find me. I'll never forget that Sunday morning as I ran, slowly, across the desert, my only company, the occasional jets high up in the blue sky. It was overwhelmingly peaceful. Then, there was a white van with Oregon plates, breezing by me, out of nowhere. They didn't even seem to notice me. Then, the white dot, now on the horizon, stopped. As I caught up to it, I made out three men and I heard "pop, echo, pop, pop." They were all in shooting stances and were knocking off bottles on the side of the road. My fastest pace of the entire Trans-Am was that sprint back to the mobile home.

What the hills of the northeast did to my times, I made up for in the flatlands and the desert. Fifteen to 18 hour days were tough on the soul, but they had to be done and still, the Rockies were there, waiting with outstretched arms.

Jimmy, the driver, having a little snore

13

Back The Other Way?

For nearly a thousand miles, it's in the back of your mind, a mass of rock that jets up toward the sky, forming a great barrier to the west coast, The Rockies. Speeding towards them, I was anxious. How high would they be? How would the altitude hit me? Then, on the horizon, like low lying clouds, they appeared. I was scared. They were every bit as big as I had imagined and they were so majestic. You couldn't help but be inspired by them. When I started up, it was like climbing up the sky.

When I reached Estes Park, Colorado, I knew the real climbing had only just begun. I kept my focus on the small things and climbed one step at a time. It was never more obvious that a million-mile journey is made up of single steps, than when I was climbing those steep towers.

"You'll have to come back at six in the morning and if it isn't open, then, you'll have to wait till the end of winter." Those words cut me in two. There was a great storm coming over us and the park was closing. It was 5 p.m. and the sky was bruised a purple black. "You'll have to go to Denver to cross the Rockies," the park ranger said. It was all over, just like that. "I'll go through," I said, "I'm on a mission. I come all the way from New York." "Then, I will arrest you," he pointed a finger at me.

Back in the Winnebago, I was restless. This was a one shot deal. If it was open in the morning, everything was salvageable, if not, it was all for nought. No record. No way. Even if I had taken an ocean of pills, I couldn't have slept that night. The luck of the Irish couldn't help me with that either, but thank God, those gates were open the next morning at 6 a.m. That was the biggest relief of my life. It was if the river Jordan had parted and I ran through as if I were chased by a plague of Egyptians.

From there, I realized, I was only at the foot of the mountains. It only got higher and higher. There were signs everywhere. They scared the hell out of me. "Beware of Bears," "Beware of runaway trucks," "Beware of falling rocks," "BEWARE." There was danger at every turn. If you run in the middle of the road, a truck could come around a turn and flatten you like a flapjack. Run on the side, and you look down those cliffs, that seem to go all the way to the bottom of the Earth, itself. I chose the middle. Those drops were too much.

The trailer

When we reached the summit, we all came out and planted an Irish flag as if we were on the moon. There was nothing around but snow and thin, biting air. I averaged 30 miles a day up and over those beasts and put them in my rear view mirror.

Smart running was now a priority more than ever. You are scorched by the sun over weeks of exposure. Your arches are struggling. Every muscle is begging for mercy. You become a force of sheer willpower, but that is where the greedy demon can play. The greed for the record can become the greed that creates an injury. I kept myself in check with the help of my wife. Stay on pace. Run smart.

I felt I needed something for the home stretch, a blessing. On a Sunday morning, I stopped in Lake Tahoe for Mass. The priest turned out to be Irish and from close to where I was born. That was more than I could have asked for and I ran with one thing in mind, San Francisco.

I had a slight hiccup with the law, the only one on the whole trip, which saw me escorted from the interstate. No running there.

City Council President Paul O'Dwyer declaring "Tom McGrath Day" in New York

Through the vineyards I went and there stood that massive bridge into the city. I ran across the Golden Gate as if I were running on clouds. My honeymoon was now a world record. I had done it. Fifty-three days and I'd crossed the great United States of America from East to West. "San Francisco, I'm back whether you like it or not, but just for a wee while, no worries." The next day, my picture was on the front of the paper, up in the corner. In the other corner was the Son of Sam. He'd been caught. We shared the spotlight.

I was much fitter when I arrived than when I started. I was lean, tanned, and as full of energy as a teenager. One reporter asked, "are you going to run back the other way?" Truly, non-runners have no perspective whatsoever of mega distances.

14

The Dark Side

Some of us are itchy people, curious, have a hankering to know what goes on in the back alleys of life. As straight laced as I had been brought up, my ferocious curiosity for life took me into dangerous waters. After a big run, I was in between bars and I decided to have a look, not from the outside, but from right within the gut of the underworld.

In the '80s, I was waiting on a liquor license and to make ends meet, I drove a taxi. That was a wild life. The hours of that was a killer. I took to dealing blackjack three to four times a week. I wanted to see the wilder side of things and did I ever. It goes without saying that gambling is illegal in New York. I started my training up in the Bronx. This was all on the down low. When I started dealing in midtown, I learned to know each card that I dealt. No one trusts you. You deal them out fast and they think you've pulled one over on them. Gamblers and dealers are truly a breed to their own. They are as obsessive as any runner I've seen. They live in those cards.

"Taking a gamble to gamble." Sounds weird, but that's what I did. Walking across the street can be a gamble. You can throw your back out, turning on the TV. I'd never willingly gamble with my life, but I sure did with my livelihood. I entered the world of the mini-casino. I can only explain it by saying I had an itch for the other side of life, a curiosity, really.

The small smoke filled rooms held four to five gambling tables. There was a dealer and a spotter, who monitored all transactions. Sunlight was as taboo as a necklace of garlic for a tribe of vampires. Any thoughts of health were out the door. It was pure addiction at its best.

Dealers were a family and an odd one at that. They were intellectual people with no future in the legal world. They lived in a 24-hour world, surrounded by addicts, beer, and free food. Alcohol addiction was never mentioned, just 14 eyes focused on black, white, and red cards with numbers. The customers saw nothing but those cards. Everything is tense, the dealer, the customer, even the air struggles to move around the fog of smoke that hovers over the table. They are usually quiet people. They have the unique ability to sit perfectly still. They stare at the green table and give hand signals like robots.

The other Tom

They never left the table, except for serious toilet trouble. That might change the cards. It is a quiet sport, but if a player takes a card at the wrong time and causes the cards to die, it's not a nice thing. I can tell you, now, those cards do come alive. It is a phenomenon. That's all I can say.

The house is very aware of cards coming alive. If players start winning, then the house tries to kill the cards. This can be very difficult. First, the dealer gives a new shuffle. If that doesn't work, they switch the dealer. The ultimate kill is to bring in brand new decks of cards. Sometimes, even that doesn't work, but time is always on the side of the house.

Depression is rampant at every table. The player will never, never win in the long run. The battle of the players to come to grips with this reality is visible in their eyes. Some are nearly lifeless as if they died along with the cards. I've never met a gambler that was a millionaire.

Sooner rather than later, the club will get busted. Equipment, money, and goods are all confiscated. The dealers are lined up outside like a squadron of ducks and off to jail they go. The owner pays for the expenses and as soon as the dealers get out, they are back to work. Some dealers became immune to the paddy wagon. It was just a part of the job. That doesn't mean that they always went willingly. Escape routes were planned, ropes strung from roof to roof, along with rope ladders. The fittest were alert and tried to stay one step ahead. The way to beat the raid was to have a doorman with a buzzer. When that buzzer went off, it was every man for himself. There was a rope ladder on the roof and you'd hop over to other roofs and then onto the street.

I usually just stayed on the roof and waited it all out. I was never caught, but then again, I should never have been there in the first place. Besides the grace of God, my athleticism saved me. How I wish I had run away from alcohol the way I did that buzzer. They go off all the time in the body of a drunk, but we ignore them.

15

100 Miler

In 1983, the New York Road Runners hosted its first six-day race. The competitors were world class athletes from all over the world. At that time, I owned Molly McGuire's and threw a pre and post race party for all the runners. Both parties were fantastic. I really wanted to get to know these people. Before, I felt like an alien, running on and on, endlessly. Maybe, their minds worked the way mine did. I got to see how they ticked and how they trained their minds and bodies to run around in circles for hours, days and sometimes weeks.

Running around a quarter mile track was only a concept in my mind. The bright red tartan with white lines was their home. Tents were scattered about the sides of the track, serving as makeshift medical labs, kitchens, and apartments. The whole idea was run, run, and run some more. Laps were counted by counters, so the runners didn't have to think about that. Their minds were free to roam. I got into it. Watching the runners, ego aside, I knew I was just as good as they were. I was in prime condition. Now, I had the bug to run this six-day race in '84.

Getting ready for the race, running was my food. I focused on the mind, the body, the spirit, every part of me that could be improved. I even set a scheduled goal to run just over 105 miles per day. That equated to 432 laps around the track and if I did that, the world record would be mine. My training and preparation were extreme. It takes that.

The mind has to be absolutely convinced of what it is doing or the body won't match it. All the little things have to be perfect down to your socks and shoe laces. All that training is great, but if you don't get into the race, what's the point? I was out. I had been refused entrance into the race by Fred Lebow.

Lebow was the father of the New York City Marathon and one of the early presidents of the New York Road Runner's Club. With my 5-year-old daughter at my side, I marched into his office. I didn't show it, but I was shattered inside. His explanation was he had not seen me run. After covering my daughter's ears, I glared at him with complete disgust, "you just cut off my #*$!% legs," I said. He paused and looked at me. I didn't bat an eyelash. "Ok," he says, "here's what we'll do. On June 16th, we have the United States 100 Mile Championship Race. I want you to run it." I said without thinking, "I will not only run it, I will win it. Mark my words." I walked out of that room the most determined man on Earth. Anger is a powerful motivator and proving him wrong drove me like an animal. All I saw was the tape at the finish line. I would be the greatest 100-mile runner in the world. Sometimes the mind gets ahead of the body and I wondered, secretly, what I had set myself up for. I kept it hidden from everyone, like the blackjack. I didn't even tell my wife about the race.

June 16, 1984, I stepped up to that line, a running machine. Every muscle, every fiber, was oiled and ready to do battle with that track. It was 6 p.m. when the gun went off and I came out like a musket ball. Straight to the lead, went I. Round and round we went. I didn't look behind me. The only thing in front of me was the tape. I was a ball of fire burning up that track.

I noticed a man on the side of the track watching. After a couple of laps, I realized it was the great miler, Eamonn Coghlan. He was the world record holder for the indoor mile, and a Dubliner. He still holds the second fastest indoor mile to this day. I felt a chill come over me. He must be cheering me on. I ran even faster. I was going to win this race. The next time I came around, he shouted something to me. I couldn't catch it till the next go round, "too fast, slow down."

The sun went down and no one had passed me yet. The body naturally wants to sleep when it gets dark, but in these races, you have to shut down certain parts of the psyche that would otherwise be natural. I led until mile 76, when a man from Turkey closed in on me and passed me. His wife was counting the laps and doing the math. It was just a matter of time. It's so easy to slow down and so hard to speed up. At that point in the race and with exhaustion playing tricks on the mind, he seemed a "wild turkey," sprinting around at 40 miles an hour. Then, he collapsed. They carried him off in a stretcher. Myself, I had not gone to the toilet for 78 miles. I had run non-stop. If urine gets into your bloodstream, you are done for, I thought. Watching the wild turkey carted off, gave me pause. Was all this worth it?

After 14 hours and 52 minutes, I crossed the finish line in third position. I hadn't kept my promise of winning the race, but Fred Lebow came over to me and put a medal around my neck, "Tom, you are one hell of a man. You are in the six-day race." Dehydration, fatigue, and downright agony were replaced with real happiness. Mission accomplished.

July the 4th, less than a month later, my thermometer measured 102 degrees on the track. For six long days, I ran with 31 others from all over the world. Those days seemed to have no end, but they were filled with running, determination, and talent. Yiannis Kouros had his tent set up next to mine. We quickly bonded, because people had trouble understanding his accent just as well as mine. Somehow, we understood each other. At one point, in another race, he said "shield me." I learned he didn't want to stop to use the bathroom, either, so he went right there, while he was running. My job was to keep other people from seeing him. Later that year, he would run 635 miles in just six days, setting an unbelievable bar for all runners. Myself, I fell far short of my goals. Shin splints slowed me down a great deal and I came in with 326 miles, just over 50 miles a day. It was a great honor to run with him and with the other runners. I was so glad to prove that I was still alive, kicking, and running hard.

The finish of the NYRR 100-miler. Fred Lebow in the foreground.

16

Big Tom

When I was drinking, I wasn't running and from time to time, I ballooned from 145 to 250 to 260 pounds. They say "God fits the back for the burden," and my weight gain and self abuse were inflicted solely on myself by myself. There was a lot of stupid work involved with this process. My body expanded out instead of up. Well-defined muscle from all my running became embarrassing blubber. My waist went from 31 to 38, my suit size from a 38 to a 44. It was all pure fat around my belly. In the boxing world, I went from a lightweight to a heavy weight, while remaining 5-foot-8-inches tall. One friend said I looked like a bumble bee.

Everyone has their cross to carry, but mine literally felt like a ton and it caused all sorts of problems. I had blown up to the point, where I didn't want anyone to see me go to the bathroom. I couldn't turn around in the bar stall. I had to back in and then go forward out. I imagined a reverse beeper on a semi-truck going off as I reversed myself in to do my daily constitutional. I wore long shirts and scarves to cover myself. I avoided mirrors. When I wore a blazer, they called me Mr. Belvedere. You don't realize what other people suffer; the small, detailed nuance of being obese, until you are.

No running and no gym work was a killer. I lost all pride in my muscle. The healthy glow was gone. Most importantly, I lost respect for myself as a person. Who was this Tom? Nobody made me this way. I did it and didn't know why. I washed massive amounts of bad food down into my body with more and more vodka. I was a weight gaining machine. After a heavy drinking session, eggs, bacon, and home fries followed. Next, a refrigerator trip, then bed. Perfect recipe. From total fitness to total obesity. Deep down, you know it's a slow suicide mission. Health problems will be on your horizon if you live like that.

I had taken to walking on the opposite side of the street from my gym. Psychologically, that's how bad it had gotten. Then, one day, sobering up in a diner, I sat, stuffing my face with grease. I noticed how ready for action everyone was and how desperate to recover from the alcohol abuse, I was. On the way to my bar, I knew I wasn't going to make it. Vomiting on the street near my bar would have been the worst. I'm gregarious. People know me. So, I shot down into my gym. The music was pumping. Treadmills were busy with young professionals, starting their day. Spin class was in full go and people were walking around, sweating, towels on their shoulders. I was sweating just as much, from an overdose of alcohol and calories. I was desperate to get to that bathroom and scared to death someone would recognize me. The gym had been my savior. Now it was a nightmare.

At home, I sat like a pile of nothing, a comfort pillow over my belly. It kept me from looking at the fat. Denial in the form of a thick down pillow.

Every day, I fought with the good Tom and the bad Tom. When I got so big that I had trouble tying my shoes, I resolved myself to get it together and pounded the pavement. That would last for a couple of months and then back to debasement of the body and soul. This see saw lifestyle began to dominate my life. You become two people. I literally had two sets of clothes. And, even though I knew what was going on to some extent, it didn't stop me. I had to be brought lower. Pain, in its many forms, happens to be the only teacher for a lot of us in addiction. It has to grind you, break you of your illusions, strip you of your arrogance, and humble you.

The starting line is the finish line and the finish, the start. Your life is a circle, fixed as the stars spinning in the sky. You'll eventually get so turned around that there will be no lines, no start and no finish.

Striking up conversations was never a problem. With the Irish accent and also being Irish, there was a lot of respect, everywhere. You go into a bar. The first question: "Are you Irish?" The next thing they always came back with was, "my folks are from Ireland." "What part?" I'd ask. "Oh, I don't know." Then, I knew that I was practically accepted and immediately, I would buy all a drink. How they really liked me!

The generosity and talk was a game I had, unfortunately, perfected to a fine art; method of approach, execution, and reward. Upon acceptance of a drink, the door was opened and then I would have to tread gently. When the laughing, conversation, and drinking increased, the party would take shape. Only ignorance or jealousy would slow it down or bring it to a complete halt. When females were involved, other males would be very cautious of any new comer, like a lion protecting its pride.

As the night progressed, the drinking would increase and alcohol would kick in, and if it didn't, we might as well have been drinking water. Some drinkers would get mellow, some loud. Some would get sleepy, some happy, some aggressive. The atmosphere on the premises would govern the mood of the party. The more lively, the happier it would be. Music was a major director of the party atmosphere and would have a lot of direction towards the finish line, but the ultimate decisions on alcohol consumption were mainly decided by the staff. Being a gentleman could easily lead you to be a "happy drunk" and happy drunks can find so many friends. The almighty dollar was being used to try to buy happiness and whatever else is supposed to come along with it. Big drink, big food, big belly. During an alcohol spree, a lot of things happen, good and bad.

Certain music, certain songs, bring back memories of total oblivion, like walking in a dense fog of senses where the ultimate feeling is pleasure. Everything seems to go into slow motion, no worries, lights down low, juke box up high and my body just reaching for the sky. Just one more drink and I'll get through those clouds and see a beautiful sea of tranquility, where love is everywhere. As the music goes on, the feelings get deeper and deeper, eyes closed and beauty at arms length. With no end in sight, sensations get so visceral. The vodka is in full swing. No words spoken, just tingling from head to toe.

The life line of vodka has taken on so many roles, feeding the complex with vast amounts of energy, power and false courage. Tasks that are mighty are now tiny. The impossible is possible. Silence becomes thunder. Looks are nothing but beautiful. Movements become magnificent. The soul and mind become entwined in emotion. Never let this stop. Only you realize that reality is creeping back. Slowly but surely, its powerful grip will evaporate the sea of tranquility, scatter the clouds of love, disarm the everlasting invisible swing that keeps the body and mind afloat. The so called sensation of feelings gradually disappears and then the vodka glass appears right back in front of me, just where I started. The finish line becomes the starting line, no runners lined up, no starting whistle, no spectators, just me and the bar stools. Some may be occupied by other people in the same boat as me in our own wee world of nothing, just staring at the glass as if the whiskey was liquid gold. "Could I have another?" A loud voice comes from somewhere. "Get it yourself," I often replied. Maybe, I did not want to leave my drink alone.

"You never knew if you were going to meet the 15 mile a day, Tom, or the 15 pint a day, Tom." This, my friend said of me and it pains me to say he was right. When I was running, I wasn't drinking, and when I was drinking, I wasn't running. I'd gain thirty pounds and look a wreck. I'd start the day at the deli. I'd get a can of beer, maybe two, wrap them in brown brags and head to work. In the taxi, I'd cough to cover the sound of the can opening. Twelve blocks to work and the beers would be gone. Behind the bar I'd pour peppermint schnapps into a tea mug and hang a Lipton tea bag label on the lip. They thought I was sipping tea.

Once on a plane, I doctored a 7Up bottle with whiskey. As I was headed to baggage, a stewardess caught up with me, "We were watching you." She knew what I was doing. It was embarrassing. At home, everyone was sober. It wasn't always pretty. I was hell on those that loved me. That's for sure.

There is an old myth, "drink standing up and get drunk faster." Ironically, I always drank standing up. For me it was easier to see the room and check the ambiance of my bar. I called it "refueling my fun tank." One thing I know for certain and that is how to keep a party going. People getting intoxicated love to feel they are part of the bar and socially accepted by the owner. They love to go behind the bar and pour their own drink and for those in their company. I could always see the sheer delight in their eyes, finally being a bartender in New York. Once I let them pour their own, they have a feeling of total acceptance. A free drink and soon the whiskey circle will turn into a square, knowing the owner provides a sense of security. There is less chance of being ejected when the whiskey finally does its job. At this stage of partying, aggressions can come forward in certain people. Unfortunately, I know that. In my early years of drinking, I was a complete happy drinker, but I honestly think the abuse killed a lot of happy cells in the brain and I can tell you that is a very dark, dangerous place to go. It can become a bottomless pit of deadly demons with no mercy whatsoever.

I got in more fights than I can remember. Fist fights. Lots of my bones were crushed or broken. The illusions fade away and anger takes over. At home, I'd argue. I wanted to argue. Alcoholics are disrupters. Coming home drunk, you put your pain on your tongue and you lash at your loved ones.

There were too many mornings I'd come in and go straight to the office in the back. The awful morning lights on me, I'd stay away from everyone and hopefully remember to pay some bills. I'd tell the staff to keep the doors open. In the office I'd have vodka and soda. I would pace myself throughout the day and get sloshed by closing time.

When you're drunk, you talk about nothing. It's all a ruse. You're not in a normal state. There are toys in your attic, but some around you are just as intoxicated. We drink because we're lonely. We drink to gain that false confidence it gives us. If there is a reason so many Irish were drinkers, it was that we were poor. If you don't have anything to feel good about, the bottle is there. Just ask the Native Americans. When everything was taken from them, they found the empty promises of the bottle more fulfilling than the lies they were told. They used to say if you wanted an Indian's land, you gave him a bottle or a loan.

Everything in life is about tomorrow when you are drunk. Tomorrow you'll do better. You are running away from today. You do that every day and you run away from life, itself. I can remember sitting near the window drunk or hungover and seeing someone run by. I can't tell you how that pained me. It hurt me deep in the soul. Disgust. "Wake up, Tom."

If drinking weren't fun, we wouldn't give it a second go. God knows vodka is not the best tasting drink. We drink to feel alive. The chase. One drink to another. Alcohol hits the reward centers of our brains and inhibits the controls. With every drink, you're more likely to say yes to another.

There is a DNA component. That's been proven. I'm not saying people shouldn't drink. I run a bar! For some, it's a Pandora's Box. Once opened, it starts a fire that burns rapidly. "Yes, I'll have one." Probably took 12 seconds to make that decision. "I'll have another" will take less time. Every day it gets easier to say yes to it. The fire gets hotter. It starts to burn the people around you. The single hardest thing is it's an invisible flame. Like a race car driver still strapped in his car, burning up before your eyes. The old saying is knowing is half the battle. I see them as two different fights altogether. One is realizing there is a fire and the second is putting it out. If you aren't successful with both, you still burn up.

Unfortunately, the only fire I realized for too long, was the fire for more alcohol. I remember being on all fours so many times, putting my fingers down my throat trying to get relief. Nothing would come out and for what seemed like hours, I dry heaved, as nothing but tears hit the bowl. I'd get myself to the sink and hold on for dear life. My body would be shaking, violently, an ocean of waves in the stomach. They were waves of vodka, rippling up and down, crying out for more, more vodka to quench the fire. I needed it to try and make it to a seat. If there was no vodka, panic would set in and I'd look in the mirror. The monster would stare back at me and I'd say, "never again." Those were my most famous words, "never again." Millions of times I said it and I believed it every time.

"The older the fiddle, the sweeter the tune," but "the older the body, the worse the hangover." It is so difficult to describe a hangover, but the same statement every time comes "why do I do this to my body, never again." In my younger years a heavy night drinking would not compare to the older years. I could function the next day with minimal interference, but today, every muscle would have deep pain. I'd rather run 100 miles than go through another hangover. My legs turn into jelly and down I go.

Belly full, eyes closed

The next day is brutal; crumpled money in the pocket, don't know if I lost or spent my money, ashamed to look, afraid to speak, want to crawl into a hole and never, never want to be told, "you were drunk last night," or "how are you feeling, today?" It's always followed by a laugh. That laugh brings the shame to full light. I made a total jackass of myself, one more time. It seems "this time is the last" will go on till the end of time, a loop that returns, sickeningly, as the old Bible saying goes, "like a dog to his own vomit."

People with alcohol problems are known for being conniving. It's a special art, that they master, carefully over a period of time, sometimes longer than people attend a real school. It is a learned skill, nonetheless, and I am sad to say, I mastered it. I hid alcohol or beer in the bathroom, the ceiling of the kitchen, the bedroom, the living room, anywhere, as long as I knew it was there. I really cannot explain why, except that I needed it. Maybe, it was chemical or just mental. The relief was there, if I needed it, for the shaking body. I would flush the toilet or make a loud cough to cover up the sound of opening a beer. In New York, alcohol cannot be sold before noon on Sundays. I would be desperate, go to the back, cough, crack it open, and down it before I got to the cash register, "here, take the money. The beer is in my belly." When you are in that kind of state, you don't even mind being yelled at. It's mathematical. The body needs relief. The mind wants to get to the finish line, to get straight. You don't realize that quenching that fire only starts a new day. On a circular track, the finish line is the starting line and you are already doing another lap without realizing the changeover. Now, I'll run. I'll run away from age, pain, and horrible memories.

Between binges, I did run. Alcohol couldn't take running out of my blood. In 1984, after the six-day race, I was once again back in action. I wanted to bring ultra marathons to the fore, especially in New York. At that time, I owned a bar one block from Bloomingdales and was friendly with the managers there. They told an old story about the legendary Johnny Hayes, who also used to work at Bloomingdales. They said he used to train on a cinder track up on the roof. That got my mind spinning.

Many Americans think Frank Shorter was the first American to win the Olympic Marathon. Strike. Johnny Hayes was in 1908. Not only that, he was Irish American. This was the first year the marathon was run at 26.2 miles. Before that, it was less than 25 miles. Hayes wasn't the first to enter the stadium, an Italian named Dorando Pietri was. Pietri took himself a wrong turn and collapsed several times. He was completely spent. However, British officials helped him to his feet and escorted him round to the finish line. Hayes came flying in to get second place. Until the Americans protested, they were gonna allow Pietri to get away with being carried up. The title of marathon champion then went to Johnny Hayes.

One day I approached the head chief of security at Bloomingdales and informed him I'd like to run a race on the roof, 24 hours, five runners. All would be for a designated charity. He couldn't have been more curious and gave me full permission. The idea was to run it on Johnny's track and have a screen at street level for all the public to view. I planned to get four relatively slow runners to give myself a shot at winning but I thought that'd be too cheeky. The chief was sold, though, and took me up to the roof. To my dismay, the entire roof was covered with vents and air conditioner machines. Destroyed, I stood there looking at those pipes and metal units. Johnny's track was gone. I thought about running between all that junk, but no, that plan was dead in the water.

It wouldn't be the only crazy idea I'd come up with for races. Years later, I sparked up the idea to run against three other runners at the marathon distance, on four separate treadmills, in front of my bar. One would be from France, one from England, one from the U.S., and me representing Ireland. The run would benefit law enforcement. Had the treadmills donated, street closure permission, and the runners at the ready, but again failure. We didn't have enough power to run the machines. That race ran out of steam, literally. But, there were other bold races out there. If you could stay straight.

17

1,000 Milers

"I just ran a 1,000 miles," I've said so many times to a face, that just doesn't get it. "Great, but have you ever run a marathon?" is always the question. It's amazing to me how the marathon has become the be all end all of endurance running. People just can't seem to grasp anything outside of it. "Don't you understand," I say back, "I just ran 38 marathons in a row, around Central Park."

In the early '80s, ultrarunning was becoming more popular. Those who got it, got it. Those who didn't, really didn't. A mile is a mile is a mile. It starts with an idea, then a concept, then reality. Make it happen. Most of my 1,000 mile runs were to help kids in need, worldwide. They were the willpower and determination that kept me from quitting as you loop around and around, endlessly. There was no quit in them, so there couldn't be in me.

In 1988, I ran my first 1,000-mile race, the World Championship 1,000 miler. It was coordinated by Sri Chinmoy and took place in Corona Park, Queens. I had the pleasure, again, of being constantly lapped by Yiannis Kouros, but so was everyone else. I finished in 16 days and wanted more.

The following year, I organized a solo run around the Reservoir in Central Park. It was as if the Trans-America race was back, but it was in my backyard. The Parks Commission had a hard time picturing it, a man circling the reservoir 744 times to benefit "Project Children." They were going to deny me a permit to have a sleeping vehicle. I said, "I'm doing the run, then, anyway, a 1,000 miles and I'll sleep on the bench. That will look real nice on the TV." I got the permit.

I had a mobile home set up by the track and a self-built wooden booth, equipped with electricity and a phone. We set up right next to the pump house, where the Mayor watched on each day. Not the Mayor of New York, but the Mayor of Central Park, Alberto Arroyo. He was a fixture there, inspiring people to jog around the reservoir until he was 94 years old. His office was a stone bench at the south end of the reservoir, on the track side of the pump house.

Project Children arriving in New York from Northern Ireland

A quick note on the pump house. If you go down into the pump room, there is a path that goes all the way across the reservoir, that sits about 6 inches under the water. Usually that whole area towards the middle is covered with geese. At that time "Batman" the movie was a big hit and I talked my friend into putting on a costume, and with all the press and onlookers out there, jetting out of the pump house and running out to the middle and back as if he were running on top of the water. It would have been a great effect, but he chickened out.

I've completed five 1,000 mile runs. Three in Central Park were for the Pediatric Division at Memorial Sloan. One was for Project Children, also in Central Park, and the other was for UNICEF in Flushing Meadow Queens. Four years in a row, I ran a 1,000 miler in Central Park and that track is the greatest on Earth to me. Each time, the city gave me permission for my camper and booth and the runners shared their sacred space with me. To the city and the runners and volunteers, you will forever have my deepest thanks.

New York came out for the runs, big time. I had hundreds of people involved when it was said and done, volunteers, runners, and service men. The police were vital. They were so eager to help out with an event to help "Project Children," a fantastic charity that helps impoverished children from Northern Ireland find summer homes in America. On my second night, I needed them. Around 2 a.m., running on the north side of the track, I saw a figure making a series of wild swinging motions. As I got closer, it was a deranged man, swinging a sickle, roaring, "I want to kill the world." I passed by him and said, "you won't kill me." I then got the police to help him out.

Every day was, at a minimum, 16 to 18 hours on the track. Rests were up to a half hour at a time. At that level of fitness, recovery can be rapid. Still, it was a bit of a shock every time my wife got me up, "wake up, Tom, it's time to go." I would sit on the side of the bed with a cup of tea and a slice of homemade bread, muttering, "why in the world am I running around in circles?" There were few smiles to be had and even less compliments. Fatigue, on everybody's part, was the special of the day, day after day, after day.

You feel quite the nut, running around, endlessly, with your mind in a complete state of war with the idea of quitting. Everything can make you want to quit. Rain brought massive puddles and you had to constantly zigzag. Other runners on the track, most taking up the middle spot, forced me to always run on the outside. You know you are doing extra distance, but it can't be avoided. Actually, they were a welcome presence. From 5 a.m. to 9 a.m., the track was crowded, then would slow down till 4 p.m. The after-work energy was powerful. I always made sure I was on the track in the evenings. I hated to see them leave. It got so incredibly lonely out there at night. The lamps would flicker off and on, in no particular order. Only a few runners would be around at that point, but soon, the rodents drove them off. The four-legged runners don't run in circles, they dart across the track in a straight line and always right in front of you. It was like you were tripping a wire that set the next one, then the next one off on a sprint to get across the track without getting stepped on. Sometimes I thought they were playing games with me. The female runners, especially, didn't like them, and you soon found yourself completely alone. The noise of Fifth Avenue would die down. One by one, each building would get darker and an overwhelming sense of being alone would come over me. It was a sad and lovely time with the Manhattan skyline shining to the heavens in the background. Many times, for no reason, tears would come pouring out. I could never figure it out. It wasn't brought on by pain, but pure loneliness and joy.

Her name was the "reservoir cat." She was wild and liked to sit back behind the wire fence. Many attempts were made by various people to catch her, but she wouldn't be had. We had conversations together I could never translate. Raccoons were occasional visitors, moping along from trash can to trash can. Ducks and their babies floated escort beside sun bathing turtles. My favorites had to be the dogs chasing after the squirrels. The ultimate exercise in futility. Time after time, they would smash into a tree only to come up a few inches short.

Like all runs, the most unpredictable animals were people. "Tom, do you mind if I go ahead? You're a bit slow for me," were his famous last words. He was an Irish friend of mine, come over to run a bit to encourage me. Off he went into the 90-degree heat, pumping his legs. A half a mile on down, I found him lying on the track, sweating like no tomorrow. I had to get some help and get him escorted away for some medical attention. One day, a striking character stopped by on his bike. "Hey, what's going on?" he asked. When I told him, he shook his head, "only an Irishman would do that." He was John F. Kennedy, Jr.

Another day, I ran into Kevin Costner, or more accurately, his crew. I didn't know who they were or what the devil was going on, but suddenly a whole swarm of people were setting up tents and poles and cameras all over my damn track. They told me to leave. I said "listen, I will run through you." They stepped aside and I was glad. I remember clearly, it was mile 743. Somehow, Costner found out my name and mission straight away and when I came around the next time, he was there.

"Well done, Tom. 744," he said.

The finish of the six day run, Randall's Island

18

Racing

When I was younger, every race I entered, I entered to win. It was not the medal at the finish. It was not the pat on the back or the congratulations. It was a force, a determination within me. In most of my races, I finished in the top four, clocking a win in Ireland's first ever 24-hour race. At that level, in every stride there has to be a natural power or greed to win. It's either in your bloodstream and your guts or it isn't.

Ives Pol was a great runner. For him, the real challenge was to do everything backwards. That was the way his mind worked. He ran backwards. He did marathons, 24-hour races, you name it, he did it, all in reverse. He clocked a 3:57 marathon and a 160km 24-hour, running the opposite way man was made to do it.

One New year's Eve, I ran a cable from my basement to a treadmill I'd set up on the curb in front of my bar. I challenged Ives to do a marathon on it, backwards, for all the passersby to see. He was up for it and let me tell you, he had the determination to do it. He was a sight. The customers would go up with a pint in hand and cheer him on. The Frenchman took just five hours, finishing up right after midnight.

Determination is the engine of motivation. The more determined you are, the more motivated you get. Tie your shoes with knots of determination and you'll run with confidence and power. The race of determination often runs its race before the starting line. The thought of running; the pain involved, the soreness, the heat, the humidity, can leave you "sore before the wound." The biggest word in Parliament is "if," and struggles are left to a tomorrow that never seems to come. So it is with the individual. Tomorrow, I will eat better. Tomorrow, I'll exercise. No, I'm not ready for that race, yet. Now is the time. The hardest part to anything is putting on the shoes.

The test is the race of life. If you have the determination to push through obstacles in a grueling run, you will have the power to do the same in real life. Defeat will come. Count on it. Slowing down to a stop was crushing. The mind, the lack of determination beat my body and my training. Do you keep going or don't you? Can you accept walking for a bit or have you been totally defeated in your mind? Yes, it breaks your heart and what's wrong with that? If you've never had your heart broken, you can't know when love is alive. "Seek and Ye shall find." Walk, crawl, do whatever you have to do, just don't give up. Ben Gazzara made acting simple. He said "show up on time and keep showing up." Bruce Lee said "defeat is only another chance to learn." It's all education. There will be a tomorrow, if you don't give up on today.

The actual sport of ultra running can be lonely and boring, but if the desire is in the mind, you never run alone. It is a mental and physical balancing act. They race each other in me, the body along with the intensity of the mind. One pushes the other and carries you to the finish line. That dynamic has seen me through 24-hour races up to 3,000 miles, all the way across the U.S. To that I also add, that I was fortunate.

We are born with a boss, our body. Some would say it's because I'm Irish, but it took me 30 years to realize, that you've got to listen to it. It can turn a whisper into a deafening roar. You can make the muscles angry if you are not careful. In a 48-hour race in Pennsylvania, set on an indoor 200-meter track, my arches fell. I quietly walked into the dressing room and put on my suit. Out I walked and a man, apparently in charge of something with the race, asked me, "who are you?" I said, "Tom McGrath. Who are you?" He squinted, "you are not Tom McGrath. He is in the race." I just had to smile. The body is the boss. It can't get fired and it only goes back to work when it's time. It demands and will get healing time. Muscles only accept treatment, not currency. You have to respect that or pay the price. A tingle can explode into a major injury in a heartbeat, if you ignore the signs. Now, my training runs are my races and the starting line is my front door. My body and mind are the only competitors and good health is the gold medal.

My support: daughter Kelli and wife Mena

Drinking and running are so similar, yet they are polar opposites of each other. They both can make you feel good. They can be done alone or with people. They also can be done to the extreme. It's so hard to start running. Excuses come in swarms. The ultrarunner Dink Taylor often says "if you are looking for an excuse, any one will do." In turn, it is so easy to stop, to quit. A whole plague of ideas fills your head, false justifications, unrealistic plans, ludicrous thoughts that the couch and ice cream are what you really need. Drinking on the other hand, is a breeze to start. You can think of a million reasons why, today, you need a drink: You've earned it, one won't hurt you, you've had a bad day, you've had a good day. The list goes on. But, if you have a problem with drink, the way millions across this planet do, it is a nightmare to stop. You will tell yourself anything to keep going. Nothing can deter you once you've crossed over into complete drunkenness. I was good at both these exercises, but one was an exercise of complete futility. I had the determination to start, but not the willpower to stop.

"Knowing is half the battle" is an all-too-familiar phrase. What they don't tell you is that it's not an uphill/downhill trip. Many people know they have a problem, but can't find the determination to quit. Winning the first half doesn't guarantee you'll win the second. The key is the ballgame. Halves are illusions to help motivate you. Determination is the only thing that can get you through. I had determination in heaps. What I didn't have was the understanding to stop. I had all the skills to finish the game, to change, but I didn't fully realize that I was losing the first half. What does it really take to wake up? When my mind goes back, I can hear my friends, my family, myself saying, "Stop Tom, please, please, stop. Just stop."

But sadly, I couldn't.

19

The Power Of Alcohol

One summer afternoon, this young Irish girl from County Monaghan, who had arrived in New York just hours before, asked me for a job and I said, "can you start now?" "Of course," she said, "but I've never done bar work in New York." My answer was don't worry. If you charge too much or they don't like their drink, they will let you know. If you charge too little, they will say nothing and enjoy the drink. After a few hours I returned to my bar, located on the Upper East Side, only to find the bar busy and quite a few law enforcement agents there. They were all having a party and everything was under control. There was a great atmosphere behind the bar.

I had a large glass container behind the bar with a pouring spout. There was 12 liters of vodka and pineapple curing to perfection. Having had quite a few, I offered everybody a vodka pineapple sample. One law guy tasted it and called me over immediately. He had a bad tone, "Tom, why are you serving this to the public? It's cow's, sheep's, and goat's piss all mixed up." Those were his words. "Furthermore," he added, "if you don't get rid of it, I will." I was astonished, but said, "go ahead." I still took it as a joke. He then told the customers to move aside, the bartender to duck, and he pulled out his gun and blew the bottle right off the shelf.

The little Irish girl, white as a ghost, poked her head up and said, "can I come up now?" I told her, "see, in America, if they don't like the drink, they blow it right off the shelf." She got up and ran right out that door and to this day, I've never seen nor heard from her.

I went behind the bar, cleaned up the mess, got the shooter out of the bar and a good time was had by all. The power of alcohol is almighty.

On another afternoon, I was tasked with taking my wife to the airport, while a babysitter was taking care of Kelli, my daughter. The wife was heading back to Ireland for a while and after dropping her off, I thought I'd have a drink. I was close to the old neighborhood in Queens, so I started making the rounds. At one of my old spots, I was at the end of the bar enjoying a cold one and the chit chat. A man comes in and points what looks like a newspaper at the bartender and orders her to give him all the money, including coins. The whole bar came to a standstill like the old record scratch moment in the movies. The lady behind the bar was scared as could be. She started handing him bills. Then, she moved onto the coins. She was nervous and dropped a pack of quarters. They spilled out all over the floor. The guy roared an expletive and bent down to pick some up. That's when I came at him and drove my fist right into his jaw. He went down. The money flew everywhere and a gun went spurting out to the corner. The whole bar jumped the guy. I just ran out and didn't turn back. I wonder how much of my guts in that moment was the alcohol.

Charles Joughin was the chief baker on the Titanic. When they first hit the iceberg, Charles headed down and had a few drinks in his cabin. He came back up and helped with the effort to get furniture and what not into the water as flotation devices. He then had some more booze. In fact, he stayed on, helping everyone, until there were no more lifeboats. When the ship broke in two and the back end went up in the air like a cork, Charles was on the back. He said the ship slid into the water like he was taking an elevator. He didn't even get his hair wet. He just stepped off. For the next two hours, he treaded water. The alcohol in his blood kept him alive. Most people didn't last 15 minutes in that water. When the Carpathia came, Charles said he wasn't even cold.

During my life, I've had quite a few near death experiences. Some self-inflicted, others an act of God, but on Jan. 11, 1988, one popped up that I'll never forget. It was my daughter's ninth birthday and her school friend, Patricia, was over for a little party. Both were watching "Alf," the TV show from the '80s with the furry little bugbear looking creature. Never understood that show, but that's beside the point. I noticed something strange in the air. My daughter has a comedic streak. She comes back with "dad, I didn't fart. It was Patricia." Of course Patricia denied that. It was the most horrible stench that hit me in my entire life. I turned and saw my wife, Mena, almost about to pass out. Then hell broke loose. Windows blasted out. People were screaming "help, help." I knew then, the building was on fire.

My first move was a mistake. I opened the door. Never do that unless you are ready to make a run for it. I was hit with pitch darkness and a heavy black smoke. Reality set in real fast, "everybody get your clothes, fire." Surprisingly, we all remained calm as the sound of glass crashing and screams echoed from the fire escape. Fire engines rang out with police sirens.

Helping residents escape the fire

At that moment, suddenly "The Troubles" were in my head like a flashback; explosions, fire, police, injuries, cries for help. It was a lightning storm of imagery. Soon the firemen banged on the door screaming "stay where you are. Get air. Go to the fire escape and we will get you. We couldn't make it out there. There was glass flying everywhere and would hit your skin like shrapnel. Within minutes, they were back banging on our door. The message had changed, "you must leave now, now, now." Before I could move, a fireman picked up Kelli. I have always regretted that. I should have reacted faster and picked up my own daughter.

I picked up Patricia, who was insisting she take her school books. Kelli was holding onto a big white teddy bear. Into the pitch black smoke, we went. Stench and ash filled your airways. I ran those stairs every day for exercise, but I was confused and lost. Now, I know why people are afraid of the dark. It is the unknown and you easily become disoriented and panic. I lost the fireman and my wife in the smoke, but feeling the walls, I made my way to the second floor. I was clutching Patricia and she was clutching her school books, screaming.

What happened on that second floor will never leave me. The fireman was back, "you cannot go any further or you will die." "I lost my wife and daughter," I said. "They went to the first floor," he said. "I'm going after them," I said, suddenly full of adrenaline. "No you're not," he said, "you'll die. Get air." Suddenly, I was yelling, "I don't know where the hell I'm going to get air."

I banged on Aimie's door. She was the rent collector. She opened the door, but refused to let me in. "Aimie, we are all going to die," I roared at her. With Patricia in my arms, I pushed Aimie aside and ran to the window. I finally got air and by God, I was not going to give it up. To this day, I remember opening that window and seeing Cardinal O'Conner and Mayor Koch on the street, surrounded by all the TV reporters. "Excuse me down there. Can I get a ladder?" my every sense was on edge. Up came the ladder and the firemen took Patricia first.

There were four more of us inside and one hell of an argument. Nobody wanted to go next. "Out you go, now," I yelled at Aimie. She wanted her shoes. We all hold onto something. I will never forget that

95

either. I grabbed her and handed her to the fireman. One by one, we got the other three out. I was the last one. I had suddenly gone into hero mode. When I saw my wife and daughter on the street, the world was alive again.

Alcohol always seems to pop up in strange situations. The last man I put out the window begged me to watch his briefcase and not to lose it, no matter what. "Handle it with care," he told me. I did. Later, all of us were out and in the lobby of the neighboring building. Lo and behold, there was the briefcase man, standing drinking a beer. "Where did you get that?" I asked. "Do you want one?" he asked, politely. "Yes, I do," I said. He opened his briefcase that had just survived a five alarm fire, and inside, there were no papers, no money, only five cans of Miller Lite.

20

Running With Me

I have been told that "bright lights and loud music attract simple minds." This may be true, but have we thought in the world of alcohol "the dark of night brings out the wandering lonely souls." We have all heard about "the loneliness of the long distance runner," but nobody mentions the loneliness of the long distance drinker.

I have lived in that shady world, finding myself all alone, just me and the glass until 4 or 5 a.m. There I was, an empty soul, just me and the bar stools. Maybe, listening to "help me make it through the night," by Kris Kristofferson, another big drinker, waiting for someone, anyone, to come through that door. That someone was more than welcome. That someone was in the same boat as myself. Looking for what? Waiting for company, unhappy, in a totally inebriated state of mind? What are we searching for? Will we ever find it?

I would send my workers home and drink. The bottle is bottomless in my mind. It can and will be replaced with another. The body parts can and will diminish, some cannot be replaced, but that logic is washed out in the sea of booze.

The question is, why would a person behave like this with total disregard for family life, work, and almost everything, except that never-ending last drink? It seems to me that there, at that given time, it is a

97

chemical imbalance or something that triggers the brain to function solely on pure alcohol.

The thought of consuming food would be like putting dynamite into a volcano. The thought of eggs chasing the bacon across the plate would scare the daylights out of the whiskey. Eating at that time would be a waste of whiskey time. Deep down in my mind, the thought of food being "a party destroyer" would always prevail. Food induces sobriety and there goes the buzz; the abrupt ending to the party feeling. The lights come on. That is always a major fear. Do not let anything or anyone interfere with the alcohol high. Never surrender that feeling. Let it last to the finish line and underneath the glass will lie a brand new starting line.

I don't know if God took a drink of alcohol or not when he created the world, but I am sure he was not staggering around heaven with a bottle in his hand. If he had, I think it would have been Poland Spring. Maybe, he got mixed up. The word, "whiskey," comes from the Gaelic word, "uisce," which means water, so it's possible. I also heard on many occasions that God invented whiskey to keep the Irish from ruling the world. I often wonder if that was a wise decision. Looking at the shape the world is in today, one wonders, but let's hope peace, worldwide, will prevail.

Honestly, while I was drinking, the higher power was completely ignored or put on the back burner. Most of the prayers would be directed at getting a drink or the strength to drink it. In the bar business, politics and religious conversations receive a lifetime ban. Without a doubt, those topics will definitely lead to arguments or even physical contact. From all of my years in the bar, experienced bar staff will stop that conversation immediately.

When I'm on the road, God runs along with me. We don't talk much, but when we do, it is very short and sweet. He's a good listener, but not the best speaker. I do feel he sends me spiritual healing all over the body. The muscles breathe his energy and love. As the mind is mostly in a state of free association, drifting from subject to subject at random, God pops up and gets the same response, every time. Honestly, I ask him, "Please give me the strength to complete my journey today. Please give the strength to complete my journey through life. Then, I give a whole slew of requests to help other people I know and love." All the names are like ducks in a row and I hope he listens and does not think I am being poetic.

These requests for spiritual strength mostly come when the energy level is depleting, the muscles getting sore, the legs getting weak. At this time, I always question my mission, running through the concrete canyons of NYC. Even though I am surrounded by millions of people I am all alone, just God, me, and the concrete.

At times like this, when running for children's charity, I think of some of the kids lying in hospital beds, surrounded by sophisticated medical equipment, with only doctors and nurses as playmates. The hospital is the only playground they know. Some of them may never see the light of day or tomorrow, may never feel the rain drops on their cheeks or the wind blowing through their hair. How could I quit? How could I stop and go home to a nice warm apartment? How could I compare my little aches to what they're going through. Their life is on the line. That's when I ask God to give me the strength, willpower, and discipline to complete my mission. Deep down in my heart and soul, I know this applies to life all over the entire planet.

In March of 2012, I was asked to run a 250-mile trek to Annapolis, Maryland by Dan Dennehy and Tom Beirne. They represented the Ancient Order of Hibernians, one of the oldest Irish fraternal orders in the United States. The mission was to help the completion of a statue of Commodore John Barry at the Naval Academy. Barry and John Paul Jones are considered the fathers of the United State's Navy. He was also a poor Irish emigrant from Wexford, who rose from an impoverished cottage to great glory.

It didn't take me long to consider. My skin was on edge just thinking of the chance to honor such a man and such an order, not to mention the greatest navy in the world. "Ya, I'll do it."

Promotion for Commodore John Barry run

The support was tremendous. Friends Frank Corcoran and Bill Reilly donated their personal time one hundred percent of the way. The AOH provided trucks with liquids and ice. The police gave me a full escort in the front and back. Fundraisers were held every night and leaders came out from the Irish Community and made me feel welcome: Sean Pender in New Jersey, Seamus Boyle in Philadelphia, Tim Harvey in Baltimore, along with Jack O'Brien and John McIenery. Even with all that amazing support, I still couldn't have come near completing that 250 mile run without the help from the man upstairs.

Each day was over 100 degrees. It was like running in a sauna. I ran beside the RV, but to no avail. The sun still scorched me red like a lobster. The tar was even bubbling up and I bit into it in Princeton, New Jersey. I tripped on a piece of wire, but somehow came out okay. I arrived at the Naval Academy with the Irish flag in one hand and the Stars and Stripes in the other. The statue was finished, commemorated, and a John Barry Gate added to an entrance of the Naval Academy.

For me, these charity runs were also runs against the bottle. I wanted to shame it, because it had shamed me. They helped me keep my eyes on the road and out of the hospital. They were physical feats on paper, but spiritual rites in action. That space you find within yourself on journey runs, that's what you have to hold onto when you're not running. I've always told myself that, but the road in life is not always straight.

Running, like many sports, is a metaphor for the struggles of life. That is why I also try to help other runners when I can. In '92, The Trans-American Footrace was revived. When they finally reached New York, I gave them a big party that year. The sun scorched faces of the runners touched a familiar place inside me. It was easy to serve them free drinks and watch them sit there, reflecting on what they had just done and how they'd done it.

Even on my daily training runs, I always stop by churches to say thank you. Some runners take a walking break or sit down, but to recover a little or get a breather, I spend two minutes in the church and I look forward to running from church to church. If they are on my route, I stop.

In the bar business, I avoid talking about my little church visits or even about my running. I think a customer with a bottle of Bud and a pack of Marlboro is not too worried about my mileage or faith. When the day is done and all is well, I often say to myself "thank you, Jesus." Tomorrow is another day and a gift that comes back to you from the man above.

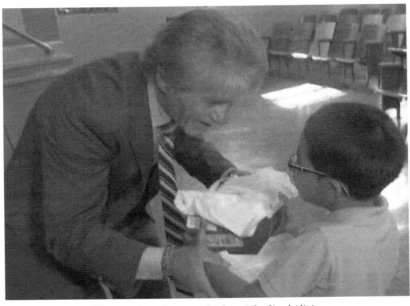

Presenting shoes to kids with disabilities

21

Sensitive Souls

It may not be true that all alcoholics are sensitive sorts, but a case can be made that even inside the most boorish of brutes, lies a child with an open wound. The question of why we drink is easy, it's fun. Why we become dependent on it, is tougher. Drinking alcohol can become a compulsion. It's more like scratching a rash than it is bliss. The genetic element doesn't explain the similarities of so many so called alcoholics.

In his prime, Andre the Giant stood 7-foot-4 and weighed 550 pounds. He would consume thousands and thousands of calories of alcohol a day. He is famous for saying, "it usually takes two liters of vodka to feel warm inside." He once consumed 41 liters of beer in six hours. And, he was tough. He could do the work of three men on his father's farm. Yet, he was an open wound on the inside, feeling so different than everyone else. William Gold said he was the "gentlest and most generous of people." He died of congestive heart failure at the age of 46.

Winston Churchill was a tough guy. When the world was closing in on a whole land of people, he didn't waver, no matter what you think of his politics. He also drank first thing in the morning and wouldn't stop throughout the day. His line on alcohol was, "I've taken more out of alcohol than it has taken out of me." He was also given to massive fits of depression he called his "black dog." The boy born with a lisp, who did poorly in school, was still at the heart of the man that said, "never surrender."

Writers are known to be eccentric and also prone to abusing alcohol. William Faulkner needed alcohol to write and would go on deliberate binges to the point where he was completely out of his skull. His publisher once commented, "during those bouts, he didn't know what he was doing. He was completely helpless." He was also a Nobel Prize winner for Literature and a two-time winner of the Pulitzer, but he couldn't give up the bottle.

James Joyce, one of Ireland's greatest writers if not the world's, needed alcohol as a crutch, not only to write, but to handle the ups and downs of life. After he lost his mother, he used booze to cope with the problems of the world. He consumed several bottles a day and was often carried home from pubs. Without alcohol, he couldn't write, he said.

Ernest Hemingway, a man's man, fought the majority of his adult life trying to make peace with the bottle. He fought in two wars, boxed, and caught some of the biggest fish on the planet, but his depression and overly sensitive outlook on the world kept the bottle at his side, as he put down a quart a day.

Stephen King never drank in bars, because "they were full of assholes like me." He wrote and drunk himself into such stupors at home that his family had to stage an intervention. What he remembers most from his drinking days was sitting at his son's baseball game with a beer in a brown bag and the coach coming over and asking him to leave.

The great Edgar Allan Poe, after losing his wife and most of his family to tuberculosis, sought to marry a new lady. There was only one problem. She said it was her or the bottle. He chose the bottle and after being found wondering the streets in what seemed like a drunken stupor, he left the world at the age of 40.

Musicians are renowned for their drink. They put the world's feelings on the notes and touch the deepest parts of our psyche with raw power.

They are also notorious for abusing alcohol. Johnny Cash, George Jones, Janis Joplin, Bon Scott, Keith Richards, and the greats Beethoven and Mozart, fought alcohol as if it were a scarlet letter pinned on them at birth. Kris Kristofferson once said the only time he got low enough to actually think of ending his life was when he was on the bottle.

Jimi Hendrix was so shy. He would carry his guitar around like a security blanket. In every interview you see of him, you'll see a sensitive soul, who promotes love. His problem started when he drank. In his own words, he turned into a real jerk, often getting into fights with men, women, strangers, or usually his lovers. He died with both lungs full of red wine.

How can these talented people care so much about ideas, but so little about themselves? They are mirrors for all of us that drink, showing us that the biggest stranger in the room can be yourself.

Another facet of the sensitive soul is the actor. They have not been immune to the call of alcohol to keep them upright, when the world is spinning below. Peter O'Toole, one of Ireland's greats, was a massive drinker. He once tried to convince the director of making an inflatable set. A friend remembers O'Toole getting a phone call, one day. "It's no good," O'Toole murmured and proceeded to dive off a wall into Lake Geneva. The saving grace—it was only 2 feet deep. He was drunk so often and became so acclimated to it, he once told Michael Caine, "Never ask what you did. It's better not to know." Once, his assistant went to fetch him for a call to the set. When he entered his dressing room, a small TV set was on, showing a local horse race. The assistant looked closer. He noticed a face. It was O'Toole. His mentor, on stage and in drink, was Richard Burton. Burton's father was a famous town drunk in Wales. His village sat in a gorge with an enormous bridge spanning the canyon. His father fell off it, once, very drunk, only to fall off the other side years later. Burton's talent on stage could fill any theatre, but when he passed on, his spine was crystallized with years of alcohol abuse.

It's no coincidence that so many that give back to the community, give to children. Kids remind them of the innocence they search and long for in themselves. Like black sheep, they live on the fringe of society. They can be in a bar full of people, but be completely isolated inside themselves. They search for a feeling in the bottom of a bottle that they can never quite hold onto. Their run is always on rough terrain. The finish line is different for each one and for some, they chase it their whole lives.

22

A Wee World Of Nothing

Once you are labeled an alcoholic, you can never shake it. A dead man is called a former alcoholic. And why is that? No disease sticks to the reputation like alcoholism. It's as if having the disease, if it is indeed that, is a crime. "He was a child molester. He was a murderer. He was a thief." That stigma will never leave that person. People who have abused alcohol are viewed with such skepticism. Everyone is so ready to say he's fallen off the wagon. No one ever considers you cured. With smoking, an equally destructive problem, the person doesn't have the stigma stuck on them for the rest of eternity.

Irish, of all nationalities, bear this stigma, when real science shows a different story. The Irish don't even rank in the top 10 when it comes to alcohol consumption per capita. In fact, Ireland isn't even in the top five in Europe. Russia, Poland, Lithuania, and several of the Northern European countries have terrible problems with alcohol, sometimes becoming the number one cause of deaths in their lands. How is it the Irish have such a stigma?

The Irish are not private drinkers. They are social drinkers. They love to be in their cups with other drinkers. We are a social people and we are an honest lot, on the whole. Perhaps, it is our visibility that has gotten us such a name for drinking all over the world? Certainly, the Irish have to take some responsibility, themselves, for this, as we've taken that fame and opened Irish pubs all over the world. Ireland has become synonymous with Guinness, and St. Patrick's Day with fists and fire water, tainted a light green so you don't forget where it came from.

There is also a darker side to the brand we carry and that was given to us as emigrants and unwanted tenants. When a land is colonized, the natives are always made out to be monsters. The Inca and Mayans of South America, some of the most culturally rich peoples in history, were pagan witches to the invading Spanish. The American Indians were savages to the colonizers from England. It is ironic that those same seekers of freedom, that squashed the Indian, also gave us the name "puritanical."

The Irish were cast down by the British as dumb, country, simpletons, that fought and drank, as the two prime forces in life. Once we escaped their oppression, we found ourselves in desperate territory in America, as well. It is said that the Irish were made to do jobs that even the slaves wouldn't do. There was a time in New York, when to be Irish was the curse of Cain. We were known as gang members and "do nothings." But, few realize that the Irish left a depression, the so called "Potato Famine," only to come to America to find another depression, some say worse than that of the 1930s. There's an old saying, "don't piss down my back and tell me it's raining," and to say that we had these problems inherent within us, irrespective of what was done to us or what we had to face, is branding, like that of a steer. Hard times make hard people and greedy people make harder times for the simple.

Throughout my life in Ireland and the U.S., I have attended many wakes and funerals. Quite a few of these deaths were alcohol related, unfortunately. Time after time, I have heard the following statements at the coffin and at the graveyard, "the drink finally got him. He hit the bottle hard. I told him, but he wouldn't listen." You always hear before they die, "he is an alcoholic," and then after, "he was an alcoholic." The label "alcoholic" amazes me.

I really do not understand the logic of the human mind, sometimes. If someone is labeled an alcoholic for 20 years of their life and for the last 40, they never touch a drop, why should a label be stuck on the coffin? Is there not the slightest chance, that he was cured? Who is to tell me that he was not cured by will power or divine intervention? Who can show me medical evidence that he or she is still deserving of that unfortunate title?

Can an alcoholic be cured? Is it a disease? Is it a life long disease? Studies are studies, but most of these scholars have probably never touched a bottle, themselves, or rolled around on the floor at five in the morning. I deal with alcohol on a daily basis. I see it, I smell it, and I sell it. I know the power of alcohol and I steer many people away, who I see heading down the path of destruction. For me, to come to terms with the label "alcoholic," has been the biggest battle of my life. I point blank refused to accept that. No way. No how. How dare you call me that. That word only applies to those lying on the street, clutching an empty pint of whiskey, unshaven, wrapped in smelly clothes, with human waste lying beside them on the street. That's not Tom McGrath. You are putting me on skid row long before my time. I'm a runner. I've run thousands of miles. I come from a good Catholic family and nobody in my family drinks. How dare you?

There's an old joke about a man on top of a house in a flood and he asks God to save him. A helicopter comes, but he refuses, "God will save me." Then a boat comes, but he again, refuses, "God will save me." He dies and when he gets to heaven, he asks God, "why didn't you save me?" God says, "I sent you the helicopter and the boat." I'll never forget a scuffle I got into in 1979. The policeman that arrived on the scene was a friend of mine. He said, "Tom, skedaddle. You are only as good as your last act." Oh, those words I should have heeded. I'm only as good as my last drink was the way I was living.

If I sit at the bar with a vodka in front of me, I will be called an alcoholic. If I stutter my words, I will be branded an alcoholic. These are all the "physical alcoholic," the outside of a drunken shell. From the lips to the toes, what name should we be called?

"I can handle it," is the famous phrase and you might as well stick more glue on your forehead for your label, if you say it. It's amazing to see what drunks in a bar will do. They will fall to their knees, but still hold onto their glass like a mother holds her baby. "I'm not an alcoholic," I roared, "I'm a binge drinker." Filming my documentary *Every 5 Minutes*, I fought with anyone who tried to label me that, especially my co-director Sam Somwaru.

When I experimented with alcohol for the first time, it made me sick. I wouldn't take up the bottle till years later, but that next time I got "locked." In Ireland, that means under the table drunk. Several of us Irish exiles loaded up in a station wagon and headed to Orchard Beach. Our licenses were no good. Our plates were no good, but we were bouncing around that car, excited to get out of the concrete jungle for a day. We brought an American friend with us, Jack Daniels. What a strong friend he is, indeed. You feel him burn his way down the back of your mouth, ooze down your throat like lava water and settle in your gut, where it buzzes with a warm pleasant hum. On the whole, it's a nice drink with a sharp little bite that lets you know you're not drinking a wee pint of beer. On the way back up, it will rip out your insides. I spilled my entire gut right out into the sound. The lifeguard had to pull me out and we were kicked off the beach. Until my gears reversed on me, I thought I was king of the world.

When you're drinking hard you become 10 feet tall and bullet proof. Desy Campbell, back at St. Joseph's, had one of the St. Mary's girls in his eye. Desy was a boxer and a huge guy. He stood 6-foot-4 and 220 pounds. He had no problem meeting ladies, especially on our Thursday night dances at City Hospital. "Nurses night," we called it. This particular night, Desy was running a bit heavy on the drink. I reminded him he had a boxing match on Saturday, just two days away. "Herbie," he said, "I'll beat the daylights out of anybody." At that moment, he might could have. At least he believed with absolute certainty that not a soul alive could beat him in that moment. The next morning, his face was pale, "Herbie, I'm fighting nobody. I couldn't beat a cat."

We played Gaelic Football together back in the day. I saw him go up for a ball and down he came with it, as usual, but three of his teeth followed, right onto my shirt. Years later, at a beach, we were clowning around in the water. I hit him with a shoulder and those same three teeth, now fake and molded to each other, popped out into the water. "I'll kill you, here, Tom, if you don't get me those teeth," he was fuming. What a sight that must has been. Desy had me by the legs and I was submerged 3 feet down, scrambling with my hands desperately for Desy's false teeth. You know, I found those bloody things. I came out of the water like I'd found Solomon's gold.

It's unfortunate that when we are feeling that good, we listen the least. You can injure yourself or somebody else. Without the involvement of alcohol, rates of violence go way down. Along with the joy, there comes an anger. Alcohol is a depressant, but it's also a multiplier. If you are holding onto a happy secret, you'll tell the world when you get drunk. If you have a grudge, you'll spit venom at them as soon as look at them.

Fighting the top shelf

I've lost thousands of dollars over anger. I'm not an angry person. I'm the guy that makes 50 play microphones out of straws, by pulling the paper up and bending them so that people can pretend to sing. At the bar, we'd all be jamming out singing our guts out. We had karaoke long before it became popular. Be that as it may, I've run my own customers out, fuming, trying to get at a guy. I had to be restrained by my staff. I sat there in the worst way, like a tiger, eyeballing its prey, as my patrons walked out of the bar. I don't remember why. I don't know who he was. Sometimes, when your heart is recycling vodka round and round your body, it's just the way someone looks at you. Then a fight starts and it doesn't matter who is wrong or right.

The first time I was sucker-punched, it broke my jaw. I was at the *Hitchin' Post* in the Bronx. We had a day of football and were having a beer, but I was actually sober. Out of nowhere, this guy clocked me. I sat outside for three or four hours, waiting for him to come out. The whole time, something was off with my jaw, I thought. It felt like a couple of bolts were loose in the chompers. I'd move it a bit and things would move that shouldn't.

When you get your jaw wired, it's a hell of a wake up call. They run a wire through your teeth on your uppers and weave another down through your lowers. Next, they tie up a little crank and start twisting. When they're done, you can't get a toothpick through there. You'd think one time would be enough to learn you. I must be an idiot. I've thought it, said it, shouted it even, so many time, because after three times getting wired like a trap door, I still didn't learn.

If abusers of alcohol are not victims of their DNA, then are they all a bunch of numbskulls? What kind of person has a good brain on their shoulders and lets alcohol make their decisions? Maybe it's a brawl, a fight to the death, "I will control you." Both sides, the individual in one corner, the bottle in another, refuse to give in, a chemical death match to the end.

I will put on paper, right now, "I, Tom McGrath, am an alcoholic," and I can see a million miles of beautiful smiles. You've said it, and accepted it, so why on Earth are you still doing this to yourself?

23

9/11

"Turn on the TV, we are being attacked," Kelli had a sound in her voice like the whole world was coming to an end. It sent a chill down my spine from head to toe. I turned on the TV and saw the One World Trade Center building. It was like looking down at a broken bone—you can't register that it's real. My wife sat beside me as the second tower fell to the Earth like a deck of cards. The video played over and over like a sci-fi movie. The planes went in, flames burst out, the buildings, pillars of strength, beacons of America, crumbled like cookies.

Why would anyone do that? We were the most generous nation in the world. Why? Deep down, I knew no one would survive that. It was a well planned massacre, calculated, and executed on innocent people. The whole world changed in a matter of minutes, while my wife and I sat on that couch.

The image of people covered in blood and dust, running, running away from death, has never left me. The only thing I knew to do was to go to work. Maybe, my bar could help. I didn't know how, it was just instinct. On the street, it was if The Troubles of Northern Ireland were back at my doorstep, but multiplied; a nightmare one might have of the worst day on Earth.

Dust was in the air like dirty chalk; the evil mushroom looming to

113

the south over the city. Fear was everywhere, pure panic. Everyone was heading north in a great exodus. Lanes of traffic were replaced with lanes of survival. No one knew if there was going to be another attack and where. Buses were jam packed. Every block was like Times Square, only heading in one direction.

When I got to the bar, I expected it to be empty. It was full, all eyes on the TV news. Tension and fear, something that never had existed in my bar before, was the dish of the day. It was palpable. Marty, a construction worker said to me, "They just woke a gentle giant. Wait and see."

The last thing on everybody's minds was getting home. Revenge became the anthem. There was so much finger pointing, blaming, and speculation, that things almost got physical. People that were lunch regulars that never drank were downing pints with fire in their eyes. I had to take control, but inside I was a mess as well. New York was sacred ground to me. Sacred.

Shannon Adams was part of the Black Sheep family. He loved to bring in a bunch of friends and serve them from the bar, "a wee party," he'd say. Standing in the back of the Black Sheep around 4 p.m. that awful September day, trying to get a second wind, I found out he was gone. He took a direct hit from the plane—658 of the 960 people that made up his office perished. A family member had fallen to an enemy he never knew he had. His family came and we had an Irish Wake for him at the Black Sheep. It was a wake up call to us all. Every member of the staff felt that loss. A good man gone for nothing. If you didn't feel life was precious before, you felt it then.

I opened my bar to all the workers at Ground Zero. They covered my bar with dust and bits from those towers, and that was okay by me. I offered them a little "blarney." They needed downtime and I did my best to give it. To them and to the victims of that tragedy, I built a patch shrine and placed it on the wall. I'll never take it down.

I was left in a fog. It was unthinkable and too difficult for me to put in any kind of perspective. So many times, those workers offered to take

The Twin Towers

Never forget

me down there at night and see what they called "The Great Pit." At the bar, they'd say, "We'll take you right in to The Pit."

Even though I think of myself as a strong man, I couldn't do it. I must have given a thousand reasons, but in truth, I was scared. That spot scared me to the core. So much horror in one place. But, it wasn't always

115

that way.

Every day, I said hello to them on my runs. They stood in mist on many mornings, but were glorious, when you got up to them. People from all nations were all around you, so many languages and cultures you couldn't understand, but they had one thing in common. They all looked up at those gems in awe. That was what New York and America were about.

He had a cart, there. Coffee and a butter roll for $1. I could smell it blocks away, my energy spot. He was not from America, but he was a New Yorker. He greeted me, always, with a smile and always remembered my name. I wish I knew his. All I can say, in the humblest of words is "we do not know who made the water, but it certainly wasn't the fish."

24

Jail

"Commit the crime, do the time." That old saying is true. Consequences follow actions. It's hard to admit, but intoxicated or not, I let the animal instinct in me come out on occasion and it landed me in the slammer. No, I never did anything too serious, but it did warrant the old cuffs.

A jail is a hotel of horrors. It is the lowest of the low, where the human body becomes a rotten piece of meat. It is disgusting and demoralizing in equal parts; feces in the corners, urine on the floor, animals looking through bars. The jails in New York made the ones in San Francisco seem a five-star hotel. It hurt me more to be there. New York is my proud home.

It was one night in the late '80s and a couple and I were having a good time. We were drinking and listening to music and all was well. Then, they stepped into the car to go home and I wasn't having it. I tried to grab the keys off the guy and a scuffle erupted. Punches flew along with my better judgment. Cops, like school teachers, take no explanations, and off we went to jail, all three of us. I was put in the "tombs," downtown, with 50 other jailbirds in a holding pen. Most of them looked like gym trainers, muscled up, roaring and screaming and pushing and shoving. I stayed in the corner, one that was actually clean, and held timid. It amazed me that they all seemed to know each other.

When feeding time came, all hell broke loose. "Get the baloney" and everybody dived for a thin slice on a bun with a milk chaser. I traded mine for two packs of sugar. Why I did that, I'm not sure. I wasn't in my element. That was obvious.

A Latino group came over my way and offered me a spot on their bench, "Come sit over here. We'll protect you." I took it. I was safer, but we were feet away from an overflowing toilet bowl and a stench. That smell was pure evil. It went into the nose, bypassed the brain and hit a ringer on the soul. "Let me out" was screaming in my skull every second. The anger, the rage, was thick like the raw pure life of the Amazon.

New prisoners came in, usually around 14 or 15 at a time, and they scurried under the benches like scared rats. The first question is always, "what are you in for?" I always assumed there was a hierarchy in jails for various crimes. "I'm in for fighting," I told the guy next to me. He laughed. "I'm waiting to be transported," was his reply. "Where to?" I asked, "a different cell?" "No, Chicago," he laughed. He spoke so calmly when he told me he was in for murder. You may think he was joshing, as I wondered, but sit yourself on that bench, near that toilet, next to that guy, and then give me your answer. "Never again," I began to chant under my breath. "Never again." When I got out, the "never" part of the equation stayed in the cell and again I found myself back in hell. This time, it was more serious. "Stop, Tom, please stop. Just stop."

DWI. Driving while intoxicated. April 4, 2010. I still hadn't had enough. I drove my Hummer up onto two cars. Not two Gremlins or station wagons either—a BMW and a Mercedes. I vaguely remember the crunching sound of the glass and metal, and screams of passersby.

Thank God nobody was hurt, but I was destroyed. I had left my bar, totally intoxicated and made a space for myself to park, where there wasn't one. I even tried to make a run for it, but was cornered by good samaritans. God bless them. They stopped me and soon I was in a hospital, then cuffed, and again thrown in the same pen. "The Tombs" is an apt name. You are buried alive in there, what seems like miles below

118

the streets of Manhattan. I hadn't learned anything. Irresponsibility at its worst. When you are that full of alcohol, death is only a word. Think of all the lives I put at risk.

$80,000 lost in one night—only some of the damage

My license was suspended. There were mandatory drunk driving classes, addiction programs and a bill of $80,000. But the worst punishment was shame. Neighbors avoided eye contact. Doormen were polite, but different, and my family was embarrassed. My daughter Kelli saw them take me into the 17th precinct in handcuffs. Never will I trade in another baloney sandwich for two packs of sugar.

After that, I visited Kilmainham Jail in Dublin, where many revolutionaries were kept and executed. Those cold stone cells and the torture that happened there made all my jail experiences look like a cakewalk. They sacrificed so much for what they believed and landed in a hell like that. I had a world of splendor around me. What right did I have to put myself in a jail?

Never. Never again.

At some point, words become meaningless.

25

The Top Shelf

God was kind to me by giving me the power to run for hours upon hours, mile after mile. To maintain that level of fitness involves a lot of hard work and sweat. Through the years of running and gym work, I developed powerful, strong legs. To do so, I would isolate individual muscles and work them to capacity among other things. In my own opinion, I would rate myself as one of the fittest bar owners in New York City. That is a mighty achievement and an exhilarating feeling. Without drink, it is a permanent high. My body weight is 145 pounds and I can leg press that weight many times consecutively.

There is one demon that scares the life out of me, literally. If I drink 20 ounces of vodka, the paralyzing demon goes to work immediately. It will turn my leg muscles into pure jelly. Down I will go. As sure as the Pope is Catholic, it will happen. I am so, so, scared of what Dr. Likeas told me on no uncertain terms, "your next fall could be your last fall," and "you are so lucky you are here." I know so many bar people who fell, banged their heads and died. So, so many. At the beginning of my drinking years, unfortunately, I can say 20 or 25 ounces of vodka did not hinder my walking. The years of alcohol must have penetrated the muscle fiber. No machine in the gym will beat a bottle of vodka, no way, no how. One can build the muscles to be Mr. Atlas, but vodka abuse will melt them just like the driven snow on a sunny day.

Alcohol can become such a part of the body, that to quit can literally spell death. Your body can go into complete shock. Trying to quit, you will go downhill. If you think you were low when you were hungover, become an alcoholic and try to give it up straightaway and you'll think your own blood is burning your insides.

They say you have to reach a bottom before you'll quit. Some people never reach it or if they do, they can't handle what they see when they get there. Either way, quitting alcohol is up there with one of the most difficult things to do on this planet. "Drying out," they call it. It feels much worse than that.

If I did drink, my knees simply gave way under me. I just couldn't stop falling down. That's when you know your days are numbered. It was the overwhelming number of times it happened to me. I remember numerous occasions, leaving the bar, heading for home. As I walked, my whole coordination would start to go haywire, my arms out like a bird's wings, head falling to my chest, posture leaning forward, my steps getting smaller and smaller. They became more rapid and then I was bouncing off the walls, eventually face down into the concrete. As I hit, I vaguely remember sparks like that of a welder's tool. Nothing else. I would awaken to bright lights and white coats. "Where am I?" I would ask. "Hospital" would be the reply. "What happened?" They looked somber, "we don't know. You were lying on the street, unconscious. Do you know your name?"

This conversation happened all too many times, at least four, I've been told. Having nothing on me and my wife having to come down and identify me, was, I thought, rock bottom. How low could I go? I wasn't sure.

The demons got me, again, but gave me a chance to breathe one more time. The drink got me. It hurts me to admit that anything got the best of me, especially a bottle. Is my brain so small, so weak, so immature not to realize that this was a suicide mission?

Looking at the dedicated doctors and nurses should have been enough for me to abstain forever, but it did not. These powerful, nasty demons dug their claws deep into my soul. Only time and all sorts of help would release that grip. That is the battle of my life and it is for life. A friend told me once "Tom, no matter how strong you are, you'll never beat the Top Shelf."

It's so embarrassing that I didn't learn my lessons. I repeated the behavior over and over again. I injured myself with cuts and scrapes and with a rotator cuff injury that is still not healed to this day. What does it take to hit rock bottom? If you find yourself on the wrong end of a bottle, you'll have to ask yourself the same question.

Running for answers

There is the almighty question, which may seem obvious, "to drink or not to drink?" Does the risk always outweigh the benefits? According to the Mayo Clinic in a letter dated March of 2016, it all comes down to moderation. They concluded that there is no benefit whatsoever to heavy drinking. They define that as more than three on one day or seven in a week. Having said that, they also state that moderate drinking may still damage brain function, your heart, and your liver.

Alcohol kills brain cells, no matter what the amount. The more you drink, the more cells you kill. It can literally shrink your brain. Your pancreas is in danger with heavy drinking and your risk of cancer goes way up.

The light drinker may see some benefits in the area of heart disease and blood clots. For those that can have a glass of wine and be done, you will see benefits. It's the idea of what is moderation that clouds peoples' judgment about drinking. If you knock down 10 in one night and do that every other week, you may think that you are a moderate drinker, but studies show that binge drinking may in fact be more harmful. The binge drinker changes the chemistry of the brain and just when the brain is getting back to normal, he or she hits it again with another round of shots and beer chasers. What you are left with is a nervous system that doesn't know whether to jump for joy or cry for help.

Scientists and doctors are realizing more and more that it's not any one substance that gets a person. Do you know what every heroine addict craves in rehab? Candy. They raid those machines in the cafeteria like nobody's business. You ever wondered why people come out of rehab massively overweight? Now you know. One addiction is sometimes replaced with another. One substance, however, may cause more damage than another, that is true, but the mechanics of addiction are the same.

It's all science, really. It goes back to the reward system in the brain. The main chemical that causes people issues is dopamine. It's the craving chemical. It makes you want more.

In rats, they've taken dopamine receptors out of their brains and found that the rats won't move a muscle to eat. If you place the food in their mouths, they'll eat it, but they won't get up and walk 5 inches to get it. Similar studies with rats involving dopamine centered on a critical decision, to eat or to get high. The rats were shown two buttons. They learned that the left button opened a door with food behind it. The right, triggered a dopamine response in their brains, through wires connected deep into their reward centers. Ten times out of ten, the rats died. They couldn't stop pressing the feel good button on the right. They couldn't even stop for a minute to grab a bite. They refused food. Rats will even walk over electrified grating to get to a shot of dopamine.

It doesn't matter what drug you're on, you're on dopamine. Drugs, sex, food, and alcohol all hit the same dopamine button. This can trigger escalation in an individual, because tolerance is built up. When you give your brain a big shot of dopamine, it says, "hold on a minute," and limits the receptors for the dopamine. What this means for you is that you've got to put more in to get the same feeling. At first, three beers do the job. Then, it takes 10 beers. Before long, you're up to a bottle of whiskey. Same with drugs, sex, and food. Escalation is the key factor in identifying addiction.

Another factor comes into play, your frontal cortex. This part of the brain is exclusive to humans. It's the control center of our brain, that allow us to rationalize. As more dopamine is released, the frontal cortex is weakened. This is hypofrontality. The more you use your weapon of choice, the less control you have to say no. Ever heard a junkie say, "I need to get straight"? Every addict feels this. We know that what comes up must come down, so when you jack yourself up on booze or coke, you are going to come down hard. Eventually, you will need your drug of choice just to feel normal. When you numb your brain to the point where you have no control, you are just like an animal in the wild.

If you have the DNA to be an addict, you can be addicted to anything. When you go to excess with powerful chemicals like alcohol, you are flooding your brain in an unnatural way and it will respond by going bats on you. How many people have you known, who were socked with alcohol and told you that they weren't drunk? By that point, it feels normal to them. They've lost all sense of balance. Is alcoholism a disease? Addiction is a pattern, and its enemy is balance.

My wife told me I was on death row, "I think you only have one more day left." I asked her why she said that. The doctors hadn't given any prognosis. "The color of you," she said. That will hit you like nothing else in this world. My brain was swimming in alcohol. The doctors refused to give me a liver transplant. Most won't even deal with you if you are still drinking. In fact, just about none. They know your chances or lack thereof. They had to replace all the fluids throughout my body. Life in a bed surrounded by medical equipment became my reality. Going a few yards to the toilet was more difficult and painful than any 100 mile run. The doctors said if one organ failed, they would all go. Every second, my life was on the line and that went on for days.

It is difficult for anybody to be in the hospital. We all have memories of loved ones suffering or passing there. In the back of so many minds is the question if they will ever make it out alive. Nobody wants to be *there*, but there is an extra sense of shame for an athlete and a tremendous sense of loss that comes over you, when you have to submit all control to the doctors and nurses. Thank God I did. They don't care about your "glory days" or how much of an athlete you are. They are around to save your life and they saved mine.

They talk about the DT's, but I never had them in the traditional sense. Instead, I went completely out of my mind. In the hospital, I told Kelli, "they are buffing those blasted floors all night long. It's driving me insane." She said she would look into it. I heard pipes being thrown off the roof. I wanted to know why they were doing construction during the night. Didn't they know there were laws about that stuff? I swore pennies were hitting the floor, being scattered all over the room. At my bar, pennies cover the entire counter and we buff the floors quite often. I was imagining things from me own life, there in that room.

Mena and Kelli stayed to make sure of what was going on. I said I heard it all again, that blasted racket. My insides were melting and my mind couldn't get a grip on what to do. Run, you can't. Going to the gym is out. My body was dying and my mind left me. The hospital was like a prison, but instead of bars I had tubes and medicine bags. I had to make it my gym. If I didn't, my race was over. It took days for me to realize what was happening.

Just getting out of bed was a major achievement. When I stood up and walked 40 feet, I felt as if I had run 1,000 miles, and making that 40 feet was like getting the gold medal. I had been reduced to that, but those 40 feet had hope in them. I wanted to do more. I told those doctors, if I got out, I'd run all over this city. Each day you wake up and you've got your health, it's another day in paradise. "Fight, fight, get back on your legs."

I wanted to run so bad and I wanted to see Ireland. If I could only run in Ireland again.

26

The Six Counties Run

Ileft "The Troubles," but they never left me. To me, the 32 counties were, and still are, the 32 wonders of the world and watching "Belfast Burning" scorched me no matter where I was, especially since it was in the headlines of the newspapers.

Deep down in my soul, I wanted to feel Ireland again, foot by foot, inch by inch. I wanted to run around Ireland, one Province at a time. I wanted to prove to myself and my family that I was better than the outer shell of a man, that had nearly succumbed to his demons. I knew I was not the product of whiskey, but of Ireland and the U.S.A., and I was going to show it.

In April of 2011, I pledged to do "The Six Counties Run," dedicated to Dr. Theodore Laverty, a prominent figure in the education department, and set to benefit Marie Curie and "Action Cancer." I wanted to be the younger, athletic Tom, flying around full of fire, but it was a mammoth undertaking and a grueling run.

Everything was so different. There were no tanks, no barricades. There was love all over the place; Protestants and Catholics living in harmony. There were new roads, new houses, new factories, and a new kind of life, that lived in free wide open air, clear of the dust of violence. The war zone had disappeared. The barbed wire fences were distant memories, replaced by trust of the people by the people.

The Mayor of Belfast was at the ceremony to start the run. What a change from the days of war! And, he was there at the end. The prodigal son had returned to do some good. I had no choice. No excuses. I had to run away from my alcohol demons in front of my family and fellow Irishmen.

During my 300 mile run, everybody was my friend, along with the torrential rain. Charity was the subject and all religions showed great care and hospitality. The Irish are a generous people and will give, even when in need.

I also ran into Connacht in Southern Ireland to benefit Croi, a Heart Foundation, and into Leinster for The Children's Hospital, in Dublin. Ireland poured love into my shoes, right up my legs, and straight into my heart. The traffic, the dogs, the cows on the road, all became my friends, united in love, peace and charity.

It's so sad to leave New York far behind
The daily hustle, the bustle, and the lifestyle
There I go to the Emerald Isle to unwind
As the memories of The Troubles, that of a spent landmine
From Kennedy to Dublin and proudly we did land.
Back to the smiles, the hugs, to where my life began

On the winding roads, through towns and villages up North I did go
To recapture my childhood oh ever so slow
To see the smiling children so happy skipping a rope
The proud parents beaming with confidence, a brand new hope

Oh what a pretty sight still there, my old homestead
All came alive, the memories of joy and laughter we did shed
Walking through the old buildings brought many tears
Reflections back at so many innocent, playful years
To the almighty Belfast, I had to proceed
What I had left was now merely a tiny seed
No more barbed wire, no guns, no bombed out cars
Just people strolling around all the stores and crowded bars

The buildings I left years ago, were tattered and torn
Everything gone, replaced with a whole new life being born
Winding through the famous Glens, curving right down to the sea
No more natural raw beauty could I ever see

Back to Fermanagh, beholding all its beautiful lakes
To say goodbye to family and friends caused heartaches
When all is said and done, nothing left to say
Except to hop on the express back to the powerful U.S.A.

Finishing the six counties run

27

Willpower

For years it was said that what separated us from the animals was our thumb and forefinger. We could use tools. Then, it was decided in the scientific community that it was standing upright. That allowed us to free up our hands. Now, they say it was our ability to sweat. In fact, we are the best sweaters in the world. We hunted beasts to feed our families with our ability to run long distances and keep our bodies cool, while the prey animal would overheat.

Any way you look at it, running is a primitive action. As soon as we can do it, we run everywhere. As a kid, I crisscrossed every square inch of our land. As an adult, it keeps us in touch with that primitive part of ourselves, the deepest parts within, where the child still lives. In today's day and age, we've lost too much of that. Obesity is epidemic in this country. It's easier for a kid to stare at some screen for days on end than it is to get off the couch and run for 30 minutes.

When we run, the body responds by releasing all kinds of powerful chemicals, that calm the brain, help our heart, and reward us with a feeling of ecstasy, if we're lucky. These chemicals are endorphins, serotonin, and our old friend dopamine. The key is that it is a natural source of dopamine. It doesn't overwhelm the brain.

Alcohol abuse and drug abuse for that matter are indeed killers. That isn't an opinion. Peyote, heroin, and alcohol, all involve the person vomiting at some point if taken to extreme. To be fair, some runners also vomit, but that is when they push themselves too far, usually in sprinting. The long distance runner often feels a meditation come over him. The mind jumps where it wants, freely, without pushing it in any one direction. It needs that. Today, we need to let our brains have a break from all the over-stimulation of the world and the problems around us. Not everyone gets a runner's high, but I can tell you that I certainly do.

Running extreme distances is a different animal, and that animal bares sharp teeth that can bite you. You can injure yourself, quickly. I've run so long that my arches fell. I taped them up. I don't recommend that particular technique. If yours fall, see a doctor or perhaps a psychiatrist. The extreme runner has to come face to face with pain. This is very different than running for health. It is inevitable pain will visit you when you run further than a marathon. Venture into the 12 hour, the 24 hour, the multi-day race and you will either have to make friends with pain, or you will surely fail.

The mind has to become more powerful than the body and tell it to keep going. That is step one. Next, your mind will fail you, "why in the world are you doing this? Stop it, right now. Sit down, sip a soda, and watch the flowers grow." This is where a great number fail, because the heart has to overrule the mind. You have to have a desire, deep within you, stronger than the temptations that swarm around you like so many flies. When you are running on a mile loop, the chance to quit stares you in the face every time you make the circuit. It's so easy. You see your tent, your chair, and bottles of cold water swimming in a lovely sea of ice.

Willpower is almighty in extreme racing and it is a muscle all to itself. It has to be trained.

At the Barkley Marathons, a race so tough only 13 people have even finished it in over 30 years of running, participants find out how much willpower they have. It will beat the fastest runners in the world. One of those 13 men was an average runner, but it was a terrible situation that brought him to that race. The year before, he had lost his whole family.

My inspiration

It was the loss of his father and his father's life story that really brought him to the race. You see, his father had saved his whole life for retirement, so he could travel the world after leaving his career. Only, he left this life one year before retirement. His son saw that there was no waiting. He had to live in the moment. The Barkley race was the ultimate challenge for him and when the best dropped like flies, he kept plugging. With legs ripped up from briars, feet bleeding with blisters, he completed over 60,000 feet of climb. That is doing Mt. Everest, twice. He finished that race, not with his running talent, but with his willpower.

When Joe Simpson, the climber, was lying with a broken leg on the side of a mountain, an eternity away from civilization, he crawled for three days over boulders and glacial ice. He had no food, no water. His mind had abandoned him. Silly songs that he hated buzzed in his brain endlessly. He felt he was already dead at times, like he was one of the rocks, that had been there for ages, but he pushed on. His willpower and the grace of God, got him back to his base camp and to another chance at life.

I've been sober now for years and what a lucky man I am. I've come out of my own abyss to wake to another day in this paradise.

28

Still Kicking

Whatever sorrow is, I know I've had it for what seems a lifetime. It's a feeling of shame, dishonesty, and guilt all mixed up. Hugs or words cannot explain it. It's an inner feeling of utter pain, deep inside.

I hurt the ones I love most, my wife and my daughter. It's so hard to ask for forgiveness, as I'm not sure that I deserve it. Alcohol is no excuse. Nobody lifted the bottle to my mouth and forced me to drink.

Somehow, my wife always stood by me. Thank God. Our relationship is like two famous country songs put together, "Whiskey River," by Willie Nelson and "Stand by Your Man," by Tammy Wynette.

As my years of drinking progressed, so did my aggressive behavior. I do not know why. Medical studies may give the answer, but that is no good to my wife and daughter. I cannot hand them a book and say, "read that, alcohol made me do it." Life does not work that way. In my honest opinion, I would have no problem calling alcohol the "sorrow" whiskey. Sooner or later, that's what it will cause, a ton of sorrow with a ton of apologies in its wake.

Aggression is a disease unto itself. It is exponential in its progression in your life, if you don't stamp it out. If you don't face it, it becomes chronic. You become angry at the world, at your loved ones and most especially, yourself. You can't love anyone if you hate yourself and you can't enjoy life if you are dead.

I remember St. Patrick's Day, 2007, a day of Irish celebration. It's the biggest parade in the world and produces the busiest day in the bar. It's a day where we are all proud to be Irish. On that given day, I let alcohol completely take over my body. I got involved in an argument that turned violent. I don't know who was to blame, nor does it matter. Due to my ignorance and rage, at least 50 customers walked out of the bar. There I was all alone in the corner, upset. Financial consequences never entered my mind due to the power of alcohol. What a sad sight. The band was playing to empty stools and a drunk owner. How, how would I apologize for my actions, how?

I can still see my daughter shying away, scared of her father. How sad is that?

The next day, I was a broken man. My spirit to live was shattered. I wandered, aimlessly, all by myself, surrounded by millions of people, some still wearing the green. "You did it, again, Tom," were the only words I remember uttering. How could I face my family? That is a horrible feeling, indeed. I can run by myself, but I cannot run away from myself.

Day and night. What a difference as we all know.

Years later, I had one of those unique days that can only happen once in a lifetime. This day, I observed the life I used to live from a completely sober working manner. Not only did I get my eyes opened, but also my mind. During the day at work, it is a completely different atmosphere; customers are in for lunch, a 45-minute break, maybe one alcoholic drink or soda. The mood is relatively serious; men in business suits talking shop and ladies discussing whatever. They all "go by their watch" as we say, in and out, and back to work. Then at 5:30 p.m. everything took a 360-degree turn. A big group showed up and I can say from my personal experience, "one hell of a party."

For that party, my job in my bar was to stand at the front by the door. That was the best spot in the house. Everybody had to go by me. The sights were so, so familiar. The old times were right in front of me.

Years ago, I would have been right in the middle of the action with a glass of vodka in my hand. Thoughts raced through my mind. That was me. People were singing, dancing, laughing, and holding hands with one another. It was a total atmosphere of love. The noise of the DJ and the people were almost deafening to the sober ear. Everyone was so agreeable, no pushing, no arguing, no aggression. Did thoughts of joining the party and drinking enter my head? Sure. But I didn't want to return to what almost killed me. My life is my training, my running, my business, and most importantly, my family.

I stepped outside with a coffee and looked up and down Third Avenue. It was so peaceful. The night was just right for a run, a good seven or eight miles. I held that cup tight. It was comforting in my hand. The warmth went through my whole body and I felt something I never really had; a love for myself.

Between the jigs and the reels, the triumph and tragedy, the redemption and salvation, the dodging of alcohol bullets, I'm still alive, running, and have a liquor license in the greatest city in the world.

God bless America.

Aged 64, not slowing down a bit

About The Authors

TOM McGRATH has accumulated over 200,000 miles, running for charities. In 1977 he broke the Trans-Am World Record, running across The United States in 53 days and then in '96 he was chosen as a torch bearer for the 'Olympics in Atlanta. Originally from Northern Ireland, Tom has been a proud bar owner in New York City for over 40 years.

JARED BEASLEY is an ultrarunner, a screenwriter, and the author of *In Search of Al Howie*, a chronicle of one of ultrarunning's most enigmatic figures.

Acknowledgments

My sincere thanks to all the McGrath Families and their children—Mom and Dad, Sister Bernadette, Anthony and Angela, Colum (RIP) and Ann, Brendan and Mary, Rev. Father Sean, Leonard and Patricia, Cairan and Vicki, Maurice and Mary, Geraldine and John, Anne and Eddie.

To the Monaghan Family—May (RIP), Catherine, Ita, Mariéad, Padriag. To the Village of EDERNEY (my birthplace)—Anthony Mulligan, John Maguire, Rev. Father Frank McManus, Benny Gillan, and Kevin Reid, etc.

To Michael Dooley—Kelli's husband.

To St. Joseph's, EDERNEY G.A.A, Co. Fermanagh G.A.A. and the G.A.A of Ireland and the U.S.A.

Extra special thanks to the McKillop Family—main organizers of the Six Counties Run, "that run started my new life"—Martin and Patricia, the proud parents of Catriona, Nicola, and Richie, whose devotion and dedication made the run a major success.

Thanks to Joey Kavannagh for organizing and donating the Six Counties Run website.

Thanks to the Laverty Family, Anne Harvey. Achilles International—Dick Traum, founder and company. Achilles Kids—who are dear to my heart—Directors Karen Lewis and Fiona McKinney.

Personal trainers—Jamie Diaz, Richie Draper, New York Sports Clubs (magnificent facilities).

Sharon and Gordon Forbes—inspirational friends.

Emer Maguire—a singing star.

Cairan McGinley—Director Foyle Hospice in Derry City.

Mike Sheehan—retired NYPD detective and TV reporter.

Frank Corcoran—a generous and helping friend.

Project Children—founders Denis and Miriam Mulcahy.

To my lifelong friends, Paddy Diamond, Philip Sheridan, Michael McVeigh, Sean, Frank, and Mickey Quinn, Seamus Donaghy (RIP), Desy Campell (RIP), and many more.

To all my "running friends", especially Leo Nicholas who pushed me through the "100 Miler"—a major achievement.

The A.O.H. and the L.A.O.H. The Irish Echo, The Home & Away, and The Examiner newspapers in NYC.

A runner, a friend, and my coauthor (whom I call "the book man"), Jared Beasley and his wife, Hikaru. You are a pleasure to work with.

To Ameen Keshavjee for help with editing.

Last but not least to all my dedicated, hard working staff at The Black Sheep: Kelli, Maria, Sinéad, Christine, Anne, Julianne, and the kitchen staff, Salvador, Ariel, Saviano, Juan Carlos and Mario—you all made it happen.

I was blessed for 16 years to have "New York's Bartender" Sean Smyth. Sadly, in June 2016, after a two-year battle with leukemia, Sean passed away. Not only did he work for me but he worked with me so I could do my daily hours of training. He gave me a lot of steps for my recovery. He is missed by all, especially his wife Brenda, and children Tara and Connor.

I enjoyed writing every single word about the path of my life and I hope you had a similar experience while reading it. The hedges on both sides of the path of life are small—staying between them is what it's all about. Don't go through the hedge.

Stay healthy.

Made in the USA
Middletown, DE
21 April 2022

64549334R00088